GURO

0010

0 _____ 5
| miles

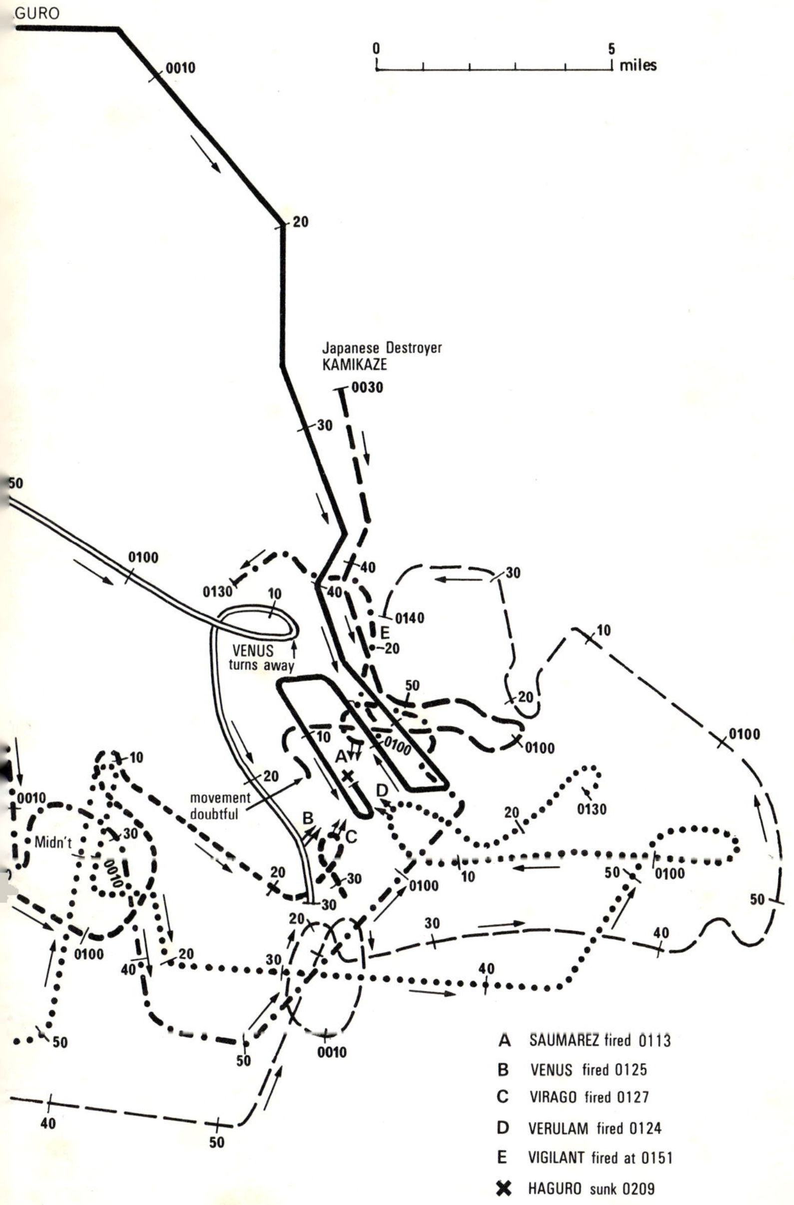

20

Japanese Destroyer
KAMIKAZE
0030

30

50

0100

0130   10
40

40

0140
E
20

VENUS
turns away

30

10

50

20

0100

10

0100

10
A
0100

D

movement
doubtful

0010

B

C

0130

20

0100

Midn't

30

10

20
30

0100

10

50

0100

20

30

30

0100

50

30

0100

50

40

20

40

30

40

40

50

20

30

0010

50

50

40

50

A   SAUMAREZ fired 0113
B   VENUS fired 0125
C   VIRAGO fired 0127
D   VERULAM fired 0124
E   VIGILANT fired at 0151
✗   HAGURO sunk 0209

Sink the Haguro!

Sink the Haguro!

The last Destroyer Action of the Second World War

John Winton

with a foreword by
Admiral of the Fleet Earl Mountbatten of Burma
KG, GCB, OM, DSO

Supreme Allied Commander, South-East Asia
1943–1946.

Seeley, Service & Co
LONDON

To the Officers and Men of the
26th Destroyer Flotilla
1943–1945

First published in Great Britain 1979 by
SEELEY, SERVICE & CO LTD
196 Shaftesbury Avenue, London WC2H 8JL

Copyright © 1978 John Winton

ISBN 0 85422 152 2

Printed in Great Britain by
Ebenezer Baylis & Son Ltd
The Trinity Press, Worcester, and London

CONTENTS

LIST OF PLATES

FOREWORD

By ADMIRAL OF THE FLEET
THE EARL MOUNTBATTEN OF BURMA, KG, GCB, OM, DSO
Supreme Allied Commander, South East Asia, 1943–1946

In the great rejoicings on VE Day, 8 May, 1945, everyone, except the forces in South-East Asia and the Pacific, seemed to overlook the fact that the war against the Japanese was not over. When I came out to South-East Asia in 1943 the forces claimed they were 'the forgotten front'. In my speeches at the Front I corrected this: 'You are not the Forgotten Front. Why, no one at home has even heard of you!' But during 1944 and 1945 the World did hear of us for we turned Defeat into Victory and inflicted by far the greatest land defeat on the Japanese. But now we were evidently destined to slip back into oblivion though the conditions were harder than ever, against a ferocious foe, which was particularly galling for the men.

So I welcome this book by John Winton who explains what it was like for the men who had to fight on, thousands of miles from home, in appalling conditions, and risk death without apparently contributing to the security of their homeland. Furthermore, the Navy had not yet had an opportunity to avenge the sinking of our ships by the Japanese in the early months of the war. This is the story of how they did it, culminating in the sinking of one of their largest cruisers, the *Haguro*, near her base in the Malacca Straits.

She was one of the largest, most heavily armed cruisers ever built. She carried seaplanes on catapults and eight torpedoes more powerful than the eight torpedoes of each destroyer. She had four radar sets, one of which should have detected the destroyers before they got within thirty miles, particularly as *Haguro* had been sighted and attacked by our Avengers. On top of this she had a war record second to none on either side. She should have been at the peak of her efficiency and was flying the Flag of Rear-

Admiral Hashimoto. She had reached the Malacca Straits on her way back to her base in Singapore before the 26th Destroyer Flotilla was able to attack. All in all it must have looked like a 'Death or Glory ride' for them—and well after the allies in Europe had stopped fighting.

I kept in touch with the fleet movements and became intensely excited when I realized the 26th Destroyer Flotilla were after her. I knew only too well the feeling that must have been going round the Flotilla at that moment because I had been through a similar experience. On 20 March, 1941, I was at sea in the Bay of Biscay with one of the Divisions of the 5th Destroyer Flotilla, which I then commanded. At sunset I was in the *Kelly*'s charthouse when the Chief Petty Officer Telegraphist called up the voice pipe: 'Most immediate message for Captain (D) 5 coming through from the First Sea Lord.' He read it out as it was decoded, bit by bit: *'Scharnhorst* and *Gneisenau* sighted in position (given) steering for St Nazaire'.

I shouted up the voice pipe to the Officer of the Watch, 'Hard-a-port—full ahead both', before the actual instruction, 'Proceed to intercept' came through. I steadied on the course for Brest and signalled, 'Speed 32 knots' (incidentally 2 knots faster than most destroyers could keep station at). Every one of us was bubbling over with excitement. It was a dark night. Radar was in its infancy. We hoped to fire forty torpedoes at the great German battle cruisers. It would certainly be a 'Death or Glory ride'.

As we reached Brest our excitement rose to its zenith when we found the harbour navigation lights switched on, a sure sign that big ships were expected. We got ready. Suddenly the lights were switched off—the two battle cruisers had just got in before us. The disappointment all round was overwhelming. I for one never ceased to regret being deprived of this tremendous chance. So I knew exactly what Captain Power must now be going through and my heart was with him.

What a tremendous man he was. Six feet five inches tall with an equally high outlook. Obviously he was known as 'Lofty' throughout the Navy. In 1942 he became Staff Officer (Operations) to the Commander-in-Chief, Mediterranean, the great naval hero of the war, the redoubtable Admiral Sir Andrew Cunningham. His staff were reputed to be nearly as frightened of him as the Italian Fleet, but Lofty showed no fear. When I visited the Mediterranean as Chief of Combined Operations, I was told that when Commander Power had taken in to the C-in-C the detailed orders for a certain Operation ordered by him, Cunningham started to nit-pick the orders. Power lent across the desk, picked up the Operation Orders and started to go out.

'Stop,' yelled Cunningham. 'How dare you leave without permission.'

Lofty replied, 'I will come back when you are in a better mood, sir.' I liked that story; so did the Fleet.

And now he was face to face with his greatest moment. Unbelievably his Flotilla sank the monstrous *Haguro*. Only the destroyer *Kamikaze* escaped because she was ordered to make a break by the Admiral—how different from the Kamikaze Suicide Pilots. But I do not wish to rob the reader of the thrill of reading the account of the battle.

I had long talks with his namesake, Admiral Sir Arthur John Power, who was my excellent Allied Naval Commander-in-Chief. He was bursting with pride. It was his job to put in the recommendations for honours to the Admiralty. Most readers will probably agree that Lofty earned the Victoria Cross. He didn't get it. Why? If he had had more than two of his men killed it might have stirred up the Admiralty more. If the action had taken place in European waters the Press would have played it up. We took it as symptomatic of what we felt was the lack of interest Whitehall had in our continuing war. And we were saddened.

Four years after I came back to the Navy from India I was given command of our Mediterranean Fleet. I asked for Lofty Power as my Chief of Staff and he was promoted to Rear-Admiral. When I became First Sea Lord three years later I asked him to join me as Fifth Sea Lord. We have retained our friendship ever since and there are few brother officers I admire more. I hope this book will put the record straight about him, our Fleet, our Submarines and our Fleet Air Arm in South-East Asia after the war in Europe had stopped.

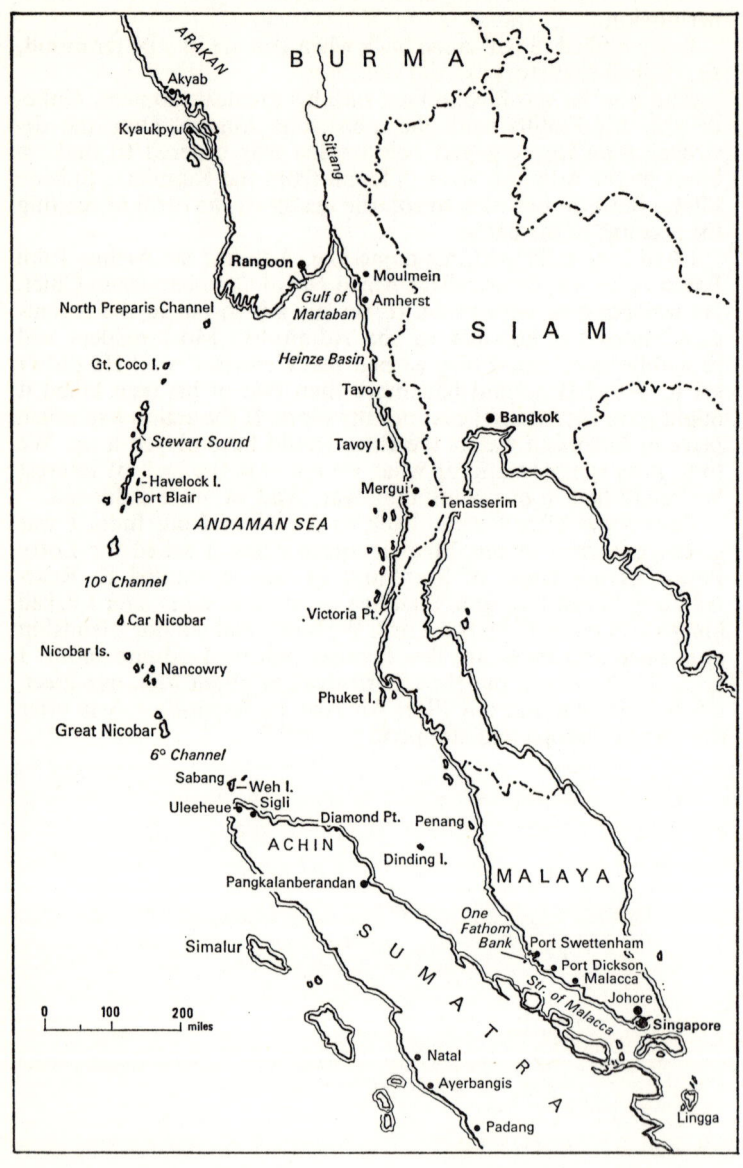

ARAKAN

BURMA

Akyab

Kyaukpyu

Sittang

Rangoon • Moulmein
Gulf of • Amherst
Martaban

North Preparis Channel

SIAM

Heinze Basin

Gt. Coco I.

Tavoy

Bangkok

Stewart Sound

Tavoy I.

Havelock I.
Port Blair

Mergui
• Tenasserim

ANDAMAN SEA

10° Channel

Car Nicobar

Victoria Pt.

Nicobar Is.

Nancowry

Great Nicobar

Phuket I.

6° Channel

Sabang — Weh I.
Sigli
Uleeheue • Diamond Pt. • Penang

ACHIN

Dinding I.

MALAYA

Pangkalanberandan

One
Fathom
Bank
Port Swettenham

Simalur

SUMATRA

Port Dickson
Malacca
Johore

Str. of Malacca

Singapore

0   100   200
|____|____|____| miles

Natal

• Ayerbangis

Lingga

• Padang

[1]

THE INDIAN OCEAN, 1941-1944

AT FIRST they simply could not believe the radar operator. On his screen he could clearly see the broad mushy traces of tropical rainstorms. But inside one of them, he could see the hard bright spot of a solid echo.

'Contact bearing zero-four-five,' he reported to the bridge, 'range sixty-eight thousand yards!'

The bearing—due north-east—was reasonable enough, just about where they had expected to find the enemy. But the range—thirty-four nautical miles—was far beyond the normal capacity of the destroyer's surface warning radar set. It had to be another cloud, one of those rainstorms, a freak of the weather, either a flaw in the set or, as the radar mechanic hinted, in the radar operator's head.

But the operator was an obstinate man and stuck to his opinion. He *had* a ship echo. There were bustlings up and down the ladders to the destroyer's bridge, adjustments, argument, oaths, until the contact disappeared, and then reappeared. Still the contact held on. Steadily, the range came down. It could be plotted, to give a course and speed. No cloud behaved as purposefully as that. A report of the contact was passed to Captain (D) and in the flotilla leader they began to plot it, too. Soon the leader's radar set also picked up a contact. It was unmistakably the same as the first. The two coincided. Slowly, and then with a rush all at once, the flotilla realized that this could—it could just be the enemy they both hoped and dreaded to meet. What that obstinate radar operator had picked up, somewhere out there in the darkness beyond the thunder clouds and lightning flashes to the north-east, was a Japanese heavy cruiser, going hard for Singapore and home. And her course was leading her directly to the destroyers.

One by one, the other destroyers picked up the contact on their screens and Captain (D) spread out his five destroyers in a formation like a crescent, with its horns curved upwards towards the enemy. They steamed southwards, just fast enough to let their enemy catch them up, as though trailing a net behind them. When they turned north to attack, there she was! For what seemed an age she had been a glowing spot on their radar screens. Now, suddenly, she was here, a giant physical bulk against the tropical darkness. At last, incredibly, criminally late, the enemy opened fire with starshell and then followed with rapid and accurate salvoes from her main eight-inch and secondary five-inch armament.

In the flotilla leader, it was the noise that staggered everyone, after the tense silence of the approach phase. It was an uproar quite outside their previous experience. All their battle exercises had been done in a comparatively decorous calm, with orders quietly given and quietly taken. But this was a sheer battering bedlam, numbing the eardrums and befuddling the mind with a great organ range of sounds, from the distant thudding of the cruiser's eight-inch to the nearer, more shattering and startling barking of the destroyer's own 4·7s. Men had to shout and then bang each other on the shoulder to attract attention. Two men stood face to face, one yelling and the other looking at him, not comprehending what he was saying. As the cruiser and the enemy destroyer following her drew nearer, the close range 40 mm guns added to the din their own gigantic twanging sound, like a great throat bellowing 'I warned yer . . . I warned yer, warned yer . . .' over and over again. As the smell of the explosive drifted over the bridge, stinging the nostrils, at least one man hid his face in fear.

Great towering columns of water from near-misses rose into the air and crashed inboard. Tons of water cascaded on to the bridge, drenching the anti-flash clothing, boots, helmets and hair of the men up there, swamping sound-powered telephone sets, pouring down ladders and sluicing on to the upper deck. The guns' crews amidships stood momentarily thigh deep in water, as it welled up and then drained over the side. On deck men had to lie down and cover their heads as the whistling and shrieking of shrapnel showers tinkled on the steel deck.

Lit by starshell, the giant upperdecks of the cruiser showed in solid black silhouette, her great slab sides gleaming like high wet walls. She had a white bone in her teeth as she drove southwards for safety. Her massive bows swung to starboard, steadied, and then swung back to port, as though seeking a path out of the ring the destroyers were holding up against her. As her accompanying destroyer crashed across the bows of the flotilla leader the cruiser turned right round and fled away to the north. The flotilla leader's careful attack was ruined. His ship was at an impossible firing angle. But soon, headed off by another destroyer, the cruiser came round like an animal turning at bay, and in one of the bravest single decisions of the whole war Captain (D) swung his ship like a shot gun, found his target again, and fired a full salvo of eight torpedoes. While the enemy's attention was distracted, a second destroyer closed from the other side unnoticed and fired her salvo. A pause, and then they were rewarded by three detonations. The plumes of water, yellow-stained in the starshell light, rose like the feathers of the Prince of Wales' badge.

Men in the leader's boiler rooms and the guncrews caught hold of anything to steady themselves as the ship heeled over to starboard, over and further over, until they thought she was going. She was hit and reeled away to collect herself. The other destroyers clustered round their quarry. There were more detonations, the rumbling of gunfire. The cruiser's upper deck was awash and she was listing to port, but several of her close range and five-inch guns were still firing. There was one more enormous explosion and the flotilla held its breath, thinking that was Captain (D) gone.

3

Fighting lights were switched on. The enemy destroyer had vanished. Perhaps that huge explosion had been her end. The cruiser, too, had disappeared. When a destroyer steamed over the spot where she had been last seen, the men on deck could see some bubbles, and a little water turbulence, like a sluggish current moving heavy debris down a stream. Perhaps there was one light, bobbing in the black water, like a carbide flare or a hand torch. Somebody thought they heard voices crying out and the shape of a boat, and another voice calling back to answer and silence the others.

Carbines and automatic weapons were brought up on to the upper deck of the nearest destroyer. Japanese survivors often had a curiously ungrateful way of showing their gratitude at being rescued. They only meant to pick up a few 'specimens', as Captain (D) called them. In the end they got none at all. There was an aircraft alarm, and they all formed up again. Soon they were steaming north-west, to clear Japanese airfields in Sumatra by daylight, transmitting joyful Vs for Victory as they went. In the morning they rejoined the fleet to the west.

Next day, Allied intelligence intercepted Japanese signals which confirmed the cruiser as the 10,000 ton cruiser *Haguro*. The destroyer, whose name was *Kamikaze*, was thought to have been sunk also, but in fact she escaped. When the flotilla, the 26th Destroyer Flotilla, returned to Trincomalee every ship in harbour cleared lower deck and cheered their home-coming. The flotilla leader, HMS *Saumarez*, went to Durban to repair her battle damage. In due course the awards for the action were gazetted. There were DSCs for the destroyer captains, and for some of their officers, DSMs and CGMs for some of the sailors and petty officers, and mentions in dispatches for several more. Captain (D) himself, Captain Manley L. Power CBE, DSO, got a Bar to his DSO.

At home the daily newspapers ran a column on the story, based on the official Admiralty handout. Some provincial newspapers followed it up with interviews and photographs, highlighting any

4

local men who had taken part. In South Africa, *Saumarez'* Navigating Officer went on South African radio to give an account of the action. The illustrated weekly papers at home followed with dramatic artists' reconstructions. The official verdict on the 26th DF's action against *Haguro* was: generally, a comparatively minor operation; strategically, insignificant; tactically, brilliant—but very risky. It could not have taken place if the C-in-C's initial orders had been obeyed, and could never have been successful but for Japanese negligence. The whole night's work was given almost a page in the official history of the war at sea, 1939–45, and in the history of the war against Japan. Lord Mountbatten's report to the Combined Chiefs of Staff gave it two paragraphs, a map and a warm note of appreciation. After that, the story surfaced very occasionally in collections of signals, in contributions to service magazines, in anthologies of life in World War Two. There the matter rested. Even Power himself, many years later, called it 'our brief excursion'.

But the story never really died. It came up at mess dinner conversation, in Christmas cards exchanged between those who had taken part. It survived in scrap-books, in letters to wives, in photograph albums, and in collections of press cuttings, battered and frayed. It lived on in a diary here, a midshipman's journal there, a squadron line book, in copies of reports of proceedings, bunches of signals kept in trunks in the attic, in an old photograph in a pile on a market stall.

Privately, the Royal Navy cherished the memory of this action like the jewel it was. Every move in it was rehearsed, and replayed, and re-explained and redemonstrated, a thousand times over, on blackboards, on the tactical floor, on the screen, with counters and models and diagrams and charts and lantern slides and accompanying lecture notes. It was, after all, only the second occasion during the whole of the Second World War at sea when a flotilla of Royal Navy destroyers attacked and sank a superior enemy by torpedoes and guns at night, in the classical pattern for which destroyers were originally designed to fight. A new generation of post-war naval officers grew up with the story, all hoping that one day they too would stand on the bridge of their own destroyer and take on another such enormous adversary. It was never to be. But Lofty Power and his team had brought off what amounted to a come-back for the Royal Navy in the same waters which they had quitted, in defeat, years before. They had proved that, in the end, nothing of value had been lost. The old expertise had not disappeared. Given half a chance, they could still grasp it and show that, man for man, ship for ship, they were still the very best.

It had to be admitted that the Royal Navy had a long way to come back in the Far East, a long way in time, in distance, and in reputation. It was in the waters east of the Malay barrier, in the South China Sea, between 11 am and 1.20 pm on 10 December, 1941, that Force Z—the battleship *Prince of Wales*, the battle cruiser *Repulse*, and four destroyers—was attacked by Japanese bombers and torpedo bombers of the 22nd Air Flotilla flying from bases in Indo-China. Lacking fighter cover, the two capital ships were both sunk by numerous bomb and torpedo hits; Admiral Sir Tom Phillips, C-in-C Eastern Fleet, the force commander, Captain J. C. Leach, and 327 officers and men of *Prince of Wales* were lost, with 513 of *Repulse*'s crew.

It seemed that the stars in their courses fought against Force Z, to bring about this appalling calamity. It was the result of a train of unfortunate circumstances, occurring all over the world: of decisions taken in London, after a long disagreement between the Admiralty and the Prime Minister on the advisability of sending capital ships into such an exposed situation; of the grounding, the previous November, at Kingston, Jamaica, during her work-up, of the aircraft carrier *Indomitable*, who should have sailed with Force Z; of the gross underestimates, in London and in Singapore, of the skill of the Japanese pilots and the offensive ranges of their aircraft; of the false report, received in *Prince of Wales* late on 9 December, of a Japanese landing force at Kuantan, on the east coast of Malaya; of the unlucky chance which led a returning Japanese striking force directly over the force; and last, but not least, there was Admiral Phillips' own experience, temperament and personality: his lack of recent war sea experience, his insistence on keeping radio silence even after his ships had come under enemy attack, his evident belief that there were in Singapore staff officers with his own almost psychic powers of insight to divine, without being told, that Force Z would require air cover off Kuantan from dawn on the 10th onwards, and his faith in the ability of his ships to protect themselves with a 'wall of steel' anti-aircraft barrage.

All these circumstances culminated in a disaster which was a severe set-back for the Allies in the East, a shocking tactical defeat for the Royal Navy, and a personal tragedy for the officers and men of Force Z and their families. This double blow was possibly felt more deeply in the nation's core than any other suffered at sea. Churchill himself said that he never in the war suffered a more direct shock. Small schoolboys at home in England came down to breakfast that morning and knew by their parents' faces that something really terrible had happened.

It was some time, possibly some years, before the Navy absorbed all the lessons of the tragedy. It was not just the loss of two splendid capital ships, although this was quite grave enough in the Far East in 1941. It was not just the final episode of the battleship era, which indeed it was. It was also the first time for hundreds of years that the Royal Navy lost its supremacy in any theatre of a war at sea and failed eventually to regain it. When the Royal Navy returned to those waters it was very much as the junior partners of the United States Navy. In a sense, the world-wide mantle of the RN began to pass to the USN from about 1.20 pm on the afternoon of 10 December, 1941. Thus, the sinking of *Haguro* was in its way a happy return. It had a symbolic meaning which far outweighed its strategic significance.

Admiral Sir Geoffrey Layton, who had been C-in-C China Station before hostilities in the east began, had been on board a trooper at Singapore within half an hour of sailing for home, when he heard the news of Force Z's fate. He came ashore at once to take command of the remnants of the Eastern Fleet. But his vigorous personality could do nothing to avert events in Singapore, where the fall of the city was, for the Navy as for the other Services, a dark and terrible episode lit only by individual acts of astonishing bravery.

In the last days before the surrender, ship and boat loads of refugees, including soldiers whose units had been disbanded, sailors whose own ships had been sunk, and many civilians with wives and families, left Singapore hoping to find safety in India or in Java and Australia. Many of these refugee ships were sunk by the Japanese aircraft, the survivors being gunned in the water. Those who did survive their ordeals in the lifeboats were either captured and imprisoned or shot by the Japanese, or marooned on small barren islands, where they died of exposure, thirst, disease, wounds, or starvation.

HMS *Li Wo*, a flat-bottomed passenger steamship designed for the Yangtse river but commissioned by the Admiralty as an auxiliary patrol vessel, sailed from Singapore for Batavia on Friday 13 February, 1942, two days before the fall of Singapore. She was commanded by Temporary Acting Lieutenant T. Wilkinson RNR, and had on board a crew of 84 men, including some survivors of *Prince of Wales* and *Repulse*, men from Army and RAF units, and one civilian. She was armed with one ancient four-inch gun, for which there were 13 rounds of ammunition, and two Lewis machine guns.

By the afternoon of 14 February *Li Wo* was off the east coast of Sumatra, having already survived four air attacks, when she encountered two Japanese convoys heading for Sumatra. *Li Wo* could not escape, so Wilkinson decided, with his ship's company's agreement, to attack. 'Tam' Wilkinson was an old 'China hand' who had knocked about the Far East for years before the war. His commission in the RNR was a temporary one and, as a Merchant Navy officer, he had probably never had a lecture or read a book on naval tactics in his life and had certainly never been near

Dartmouth or Greenwich. But, with a flat-bottomed Yangtse steamer, a scratch crew and three small guns, he engaged a Japanese heavy cruiser. So brilliantly did Wilkinson handle *Li Wo* that he stayed in action for over an hour. *Li Wo* finally rammed a Japanese transport she had previously set on fire, and sank. There were ten survivors. Wilkinson was not one of them, and not all those survived Japanese captivity and came safe home after the war. It was some time after the war before Wilkinson's exploit was known. His posthumous VC was not gazetted until December, 1946.

Admiral Layton was forced to move his headquarters to Colombo and in so doing made one of the most misunderstood signals of the war: 'With your heads held high and your hearts beating proudly, I leave the defence of Singapore in your strong and capable hands. I am off to Colombo to collect a new fleet.'

The Admiral only meant to be encouraging, and his move to Colombo was certainly necessary. But the unfortunate wording of the last sentence could only have one possible interpretation on the lower deck: 'Up ladder, Jack, I'm inboard!'

By the end of February, 1942, the strategic situation all over the Far East had deteriorated for the Allies. Singapore had been surrendered on the 15th, after one of the least competent campaigns ever fought by a British general. In Burma, the Japanese were running everything before them, inflicting major defeats, amounting almost to disasters, upon British and Indian troops at the Binin and Sittang rivers. At the end of the month, a mixed force of British, Australian, American and Dutch ships, lacking air cover, and led by a fatally unlucky Dutch Admiral, had tried to prevent the Japanese invasion of Java and were badly mauled in what Churchill called 'the forlorn battle' in the Java Sea. In March, Rangoon fell on the 8th, the Indonesian Government capitulated unconditionally on the 9th, and General MacArthur left the Philippines on the 24th, at President Roosevelt's personal insistence.

9

At this very gloomy time Admiral Sir James Somerville arrived to take over as C-in-C Eastern Fleet, while Admiral Layton organized the defences of Ceylon. Sir James was as good as a tonic. He had a splendid war record behind him as Flag Officer, Force H. He was a bold man and a witty man, with a somewhat Rabelaisian sense of humour and the common touch. He was famous for his signals and his fleet were not disappointed when he first saw them at sea: 'So this is the Eastern Fleet,' he signalled, 'Well never mind, there's many a good tune played on an old fiddle.'

There was a certain rueful truth in that. The Eastern Fleet was the largest the Admiralty could get together and it looked impressive on paper. But four of the five battleships, *Resolution*, *Ramillies*, *Royal Sovereign* and *Revenge*, were old, slow, with short endurance, dating from the First World War. One of the aircraft carriers was *Hermes*, who was old, slow and small, and the air groups of the two fleet carriers, *Formidable* and *Indomitable*, lacked battle experience.

However, Sir James radiated a confidence he could not have felt as he prepared his assorted fleet for battle. In fact there was little time left. The Eastern Fleet, despite its shortcomings, was still a 'fleet in being' and a threat to the flanks of the Japanese advance in Burma. On 28 March Intelligence reported a powerful Japanese raiding force entering the Indian Ocean, and steaming westwards. Admiral Somerville, flying his flag in *Warspite*, formed his fleet in two tactical units, a fast Force 'A' with the two fleet carriers under his own command, and a slow Force 'B' under his second-in-command, Vice-Admiral Algernon Willis. Somerville hoped to engage the enemy with Force 'A', preferably with a night torpedo attack by Albacores from the carriers, while Force 'B' remained in support.

Short fleet endurance forced him back to Addu Atoll, which was euphemistically termed a 'fleet base', but known by the sailors as 'Scapa with palm trees', before the Japanese could be brought to action. Typically, Somerville was disappointed. 'I fear,' he wrote, 'they have taken fright which is a pity because if I could have given them a good crack now it would have been timely.'

In fact it was very fortunate for Somerville and his ships that they did not meet the Japanese. For the raiders were actually Vice-Admiral Nagumo's striking force, with five out of the six carriers which had attacked Pearl Harbor, four fast battleships, two cruisers and destroyers. The outcome, barring a miracle, would almost certainly have been yet another shattering disaster to the Eastern Fleet.

Nagumo failed to find the Eastern Fleet, but made short work of the targets left for him. While Vice-Admiral Ozawa, with one carrier, cruisers and destroyers, raided the east coast of India, Nagumo's aircraft fell upon Colombo on Easter Sunday, 5 April. The harbour had been cleared and the damage limited, but on the same day Nagumo's dive-bombers surprised and sank the cruisers *Cornwall* and *Dorsetshire*, who were on their way to rejoin the main fleet. On 9 April, off the east coast of Ceylon, Japanese aircraft bombed and sank *Hermes*, the destroyer *Vampire*, the corvette *Hollyhock* and two tankers. The slow Force 'B' withdrew to Mombasa, while Force 'A' steamed to Bombay. Somerville still had his fleet but from now on he would, in his own words, 'have to lie low in one sense, but be pretty active in another—keep the old tarts out of the picture and roar about with the others'.

On the day *Hermes* was sunk, the surviving American and Filipino troops on the Bataan peninsula surrendered. Corregidor, the last Allied post in the Philippines, fell on 6 May, while in Burma the British and Indian troops of the Eastern Army were reaching the Assam frontier after a retreat of 1,000 miles—the longest in British military history. In six months the Japanese had seized their Greater South-East Asia Co-Prosperity Sphere—an empire of some ninety million people which stretched from Rabaul to Rangoon. This she had achieved at a cost of about 15,000 men killed and wounded, about 400 aircraft, and twenty-three warships, none of them larger than a destroyer.

Yet, even in May, 1942, the picture was not entirely black for the Allies. After the strategic reverse at the battle in the Coral Sea, the Japanese were about to receive a sharp 'comeuppance' at Midway. Even in the Indian Ocean, there was one small offensive move, against Madagascar. With the central Mediterranean closed to surface shipping, Allied convoys for the Middle East had to go round the Cape of Good Hope and up the eastern coast of Africa where, lying squarely athwart the convoy routes, lay the Vichy French island of Madagascar. With the memory of how easily the Vichy French had allowed the Japanese to infest Indo-China and faced by the prospect of what Japanese submarines based on Madagascar could do to the vital convoys, the Allied Chiefs of Staff ordered the island to be invaded.

Covered by aircraft from *Illustrious* and *Indomitable*, the first landing took place in the north of the island on 5 May and the town of Diego Suarez was secured in two days. But when the Japanese submarines continued to operate in the area, it was decided to go on and take the whole island. Though suffering more casualties from subtertian malaria than from the French, the troops pressed southwards in September and October. The last Vichy resistance collapsed in November.

By that time Somerville's fleet had been drastically reduced. *Indomitable* left in July, to take part in the 'Pedestal' relief convoy for Malta. *Formidable* soon followed for the 'Torch' landings in North Africa. *Illustrious* went home for refit in January, 1943. *Warspite*, *Valiant*, the cruiser *Mauritius* and several destroyers all left the station later in the year, leaving the Eastern Fleet with barely enough ships to escort the Cape–Suez and Cape–Colombo convoys. Much as Sir James might have longed for some vigorous action against the Japanese, it was out of the question. The operational centres of gravity for the Navy for most of 1943 were still in the Mediterranean and in the continuing struggle in the Atlantic.

Submarines could have taken the war to the enemy, at a time when surface ships were scarce. But even here the Eastern Fleet was virtually impotent. One of Admiral Layton's first acts, on taking over the fleet, had been to ask for some submarines to be sent to the Far East. In the Mediterranean, 1941 had been a grim year for the submarine service, with eight boats lost, and the coming year of 1942 was to be even worse. But *Trusty* and *Truant* were sent to the East in December, 1941, and January, 1942, and after the fall of Singapore went to Surabaya where they operated for a while with Dutch and American submarines. *Trusty*, *Truant* and four Dutch boats arrived at Colombo in March, 1942. Submarines carried out sporadic patrols from June, 1942, until March, 1943. *Trident* arrived in August but suffered engine defects and had to return to the United Kingdom after only one patrol. By September, 1943, the Eastern Fleet's submarine strength had dwindled to its absolute nadir, only one boat operational, the Dutch *0.24*.

However, with the surrender of the bulk of the Italian fleet in September, 1943, and the immobilization of the battleship *Tirpitz* in Altenfjord by X-craft midget submarines the same month, a number of ships, including units of the Mediterranean Fleet, were released for service elsewhere. Submarines were the first to be reinforced. The depot ship *Adamant*, mother to the 4th Submarine Flotilla, set up residence in Trincomalee in October. Seven more submarines arrived late in September or October and *Taurus* set the ball rolling by sinking the Japanese U-boat *I-34* off Penang on 13 November. By January, 1944, the 4th Flotilla had six 'T' Class and one 'S' Class. Four more 'S' and one 'T' arrived in February. A second depot ship, *Maidstone*, arrived in March, and a second flotilla, the 8th, was formed from the 'S' Class submarines. For the first time in the war the submarines began properly to carry submarine warfare to the eastern coasts of the Malay barrier.

Throughout 1943, the Allies in the Pacific had sustained a dual advance on the strategic Japanese stronghold at Rabaul, in the Solomons and in New Guinea, and by New Year's Day, 1944, Rabaul had been partly neutralized and bypassed. The door of the Bismarcks, the outer Japanese defence barrier, had been forced open. In the central Pacific, the 'Atoll War' had begun with the capture of the Gilbert Islands in November, 1943, and Nimitz's forces were poised to assault the Marshall Islands in January, 1944.

In December, 1943, the Admiralty put up proposals to send a British Pacific Ocean Force of three capital ships, one or two carriers, cruisers and destroyers, to serve in the Pacific. This showed the British intentions to join the Pacific war but in fact the Force was never formed. The formation of a British Pacific Fleet, in its final form, had many political and material battles to be fought. Late in 1943 the ships could not be sent because of the need to resume the Arctic convoys and, ironically, the requirement to strengthen the Eastern Fleet for operations early in 1944.

At last, having been the 'little orphan Annie' of the Navy, starved and deprived of resources for so long, the Eastern Fleet began to experience something of a renaissance early in 1944. In January the Admiralty planned to send a total of 146 ships to join the fleet in the next four months. That was never achieved but fleet strength did start to build up rapidly. On 27 January Vice-Admiral Sir Arthur John Power, commanding the First Battle Squadron and Flag Officer Second-in-Command Eastern Fleet, arrived in Ceylon with the battleships *Valiant* and *Queen Elizabeth*, the battle cruiser *Renown*, the aircraft carrier *Illustrious* and the repair carrier *Unicorn*.

On 24 February, 1944, the main Japanese fleet arrived at Singapore and it seemed that Admiral Power had arrived just in time. But in fact the Japanese had no offensive intentions towards the Indian Ocean. They had moved to Singapore so as to be nearer their fuel supplies in the Dutch East Indies and because American fleet carrier strikes at Truk and Yap had made those bases impossible for large ships.

The Japanese had four battleships, six cruisers and two carriers, followed by a third in March, with destroyers and auxiliaries and it was fortunate they had no offensive intentions, for the Eastern

14

Fleet was still so short of strength that *Unicorn* had to be used as an operational carrier. There was a shortage of destroyers too. There were not enough to escort the fleet and the Indian Ocean convoys. The convoys took priority.

The Eastern Fleet's operations in 1944 were a kind of muted accompaniment in a minor key to the great themes of the Pacific. Operations were timed to have a distracting effect, in the hope that the Japanese would divert forces to the Indian Ocean. So, to accompany MacArthur's landing at Hollandia in April, the Eastern Fleet put to sea for Operation COCKPIT. The fleet had recently been reinforced by the escort carriers *Shah* and *Begum*, the French battleship *Richelieu*, more destroyers and, most importantly, the US carrier *Saratoga* and three American destroyers.

The fleet sailed under Sir James himself for strikes by aircraft from *Illustrious* and *Saratoga* on the harbour and oil storage tanks at Sabang, on Weh Island, north of Sumatra. These took place on 19 April and were intended to pin down Japanese air and surface forces in the Singapore area while the Hollandia assaults took place.

On 17 May, shortly before *Saratoga* returned to the Pacific, the fleet carried out a second strike, on the harbour of Surabaya in Java and the oil refinery at Wonokrono. This was a long range operation in which the fleet steamed some 7,000 miles, refuelling at Exmouth Bay in Western Australia. The Japanese seemed to be taken by surprise, or perhaps were indifferent. Neither strike met much opposition. However, they both showed that *Saratoga* was in a class quite above *Illustrious* in the operation of carrier aircraft. The Fleet Air Arm still had something to learn before it could take its place beside the US carriers in the Pacific.

In June, 1944, Admiral King asked again for more effort in the Andamans-Malay area, to help the US Pacific fleet by keeping pressure on the Japanese. Once again, while the climactic carrier battle of the Philippine Sea was fought, the Eastern Fleet did their best to divert Japanese effort, by a carrier air strike at Port Blair in the Andaman Islands (Operation PEDAL), a scene which was to become familiar for many ships in the fleet. Two more fleet carriers, *Victorious* and *Indomitable*, joined the fleet in July and on the 22nd Admiral Somerville led a huge force (for the Eastern Fleet) of the battleships *Valiant* and *Richelieu*, the battle cruiser *Renown*, *Victorious* and *Illustrious*, the cruisers *Nigeria*, *Kenya*, *Gambia*, *Ceylon*, *Cumberland*, *Phoebe*, and the Dutch *Tromp*, and ten destroyers, for Operation CRIMSON, a much more ambitious attack on Sabang. Sir James' 62nd birthday had fallen on the 17th and the fleet laid on satisfactory celebrations. The capital ships lay off and bombarded the town and harbour, carrier aircraft strafed and bombed airfields and installations, while the destroyers led by Captain Richard Onslow steamed into the harbour entrance, firing guns and torpedoes in spectacular fashion. It was all most heartening and encouraging for the future, although post-war investigation showed that none of the harassing operations caused the Japanese to move any significant forces into the South-east Asia area.

The new battleship *Howe* arrived at Trincomalee on 8 August but the capital ship *status quo* was restored at once when the giant floating dock AFD 28 in the harbour collapsed, damaging *Valiant*, who happened to be docked inside, so badly she had to be sent home. On the 22nd Sir James was relieved by Admiral Sir Bruce Fraser and went to Washington as Head of the British Admiralty Delegation. He had hoisted his flag in the dark days of March, 1942, and had seen the fleet through its days of weakness, shepherding his few ships through a time of shortage and frustration. Ironically, he was now leaving when the fleet was gathering strength every week and beginning to flex its muscles for the offensive against Japan. Towards the end of August the Eastern Fleet carried out Operation BOOMERANG, to provide air-sea rescue cover for a 20th US Bomber Command attack on Sumatra, and a carrier aircraft strike on the Inda-Roeng cement works near Padang in Sumatra (Operation BANQUET).

In the Pacific, after the great victory over the Imperial Japanese

Navy's aircrews in the Philippine Sea, events hurried towards the Battle of Leyte Gulf and the pace of invasion quickened. The Eastern Fleet once more carried out diversionary operations as the autumn of 1944 drew on. In September, to coincide with the landings at Pelelieu, in the Palau Islands, Rear-Admiral Clement Moody, Flag Officer Air, took *Victorious* and *Indomitable* to attack the port of Sigli in northern Sumatra and to carry out photo-reconnaissance flights. On 17 and 19 October, coinciding with MacArthur's landings at Leyte, the Eastern Fleet carried out three days of strikes against Japanese island bases at Nancowry and Car Nicobar. The intention was to make the Japanese believe that the islands were about to be invaded. Whether or not the Japanese were so deceived, they made little sign of reaction, mounted ineffectual air attacks and made no moves by surface forces. In fact, the main Japanese Battle Fleet sailed from Singapore eastwards, to take its part in the battle of Leyte Gulf.

One arm of the Navy which did exert constant and noticeable pressure on the Japanese were the submarines. They took their chances, snapped up every trifle offered them, kept a constant watch, creating an uneasy sensation in the enemy's consciousness that no waters outside Singapore harbour or the Johore Strait itself, save perhaps Penang, were really safe (and X-craft in July, 1945, were to show that even the Johore Strait could be penetrated by submarine). By 1944 all new and refitted 'T' and 'S' Class submarines were being sent to the Eastern Fleet. The newly designed 'A' class—larger, faster, and with a much longer range than any previous class of British submarine—were also intended specifically for the Far Eastern War, although none of them was completed in time to make an operational patrol. The 'T' and 'S' were thus the only submarines available and they never had the range, speed, or crew amenities of the American patrol sub-marines. But special efforts were made to convert them for long-range service in the tropics. Extra stowages for fuel, lubricating oil and water were provided. A second air-conditioning plant and increased refrigerating capacity were also fitted.

17

The effect of the submarine offensive was such that the Japanese soon abandoned coastal convoys along the west coasts of the Malay barrier except on rare occasions or with very small ships. Eastern Fleet submarines made 88 patrols, mostly in the Malacca Strait area, between January and September, 1944, and found targets increasingly fewer and smaller. Only eight enemy vessels were over 500 tons and the total tonnage sunk was 15,920 tons. Some Japanese warships were also sunk. *Tally Ho* sank the cruiser *Kuma* on 11 January and the ex-Italian U-boat *U-It 23* on 23 February. *Telemachus* sank the Japanese U-boat *I.166* off One Fathom Bank on 17 July and *Trenchant* sank *U-859* off Penang on 23 September. On the debit side, *Stonehenge* was missing and presumed lost in the Malacca Strait on 20 March.

A third depot ship *Wolfe* arrived in Trincomalee on 19 August, and by 1 September Eastern Fleet submarine strength had climbed to 27 submarines which was more submarines than could be usefully employed in the Malacca Strait area. Later, in August, 1944, *Maidstone* sailed for Fremantle in Australia to operate with the American submarines of the South-western Pacific area. Their first major success was by the Dutch *Zwaardsfisch* who sank *U-168* on 6 October and the minelayer *Itsukushima* on the 17th in the Java Sea.

Although submarines were capable of a variety of tasks (in October *Trenchant* took 'chariots' for a penetration of Phuket Island harbour) the submarines' strategic objective was to maintain a blockade of all enemy traffic by sea, sinking ships by torpedo or gunfire, or boarding and placing demolition charges. For the submarines it was a war of endless heat, of sweat and salt tablets, of never enough cold drinks, of meals so hot the meat dripped on the plates. Men went about with towels wrapped round their waists. Despite skin itches, rashes, prickly heat and the difficulty of keeping clean, in general their health was surprisingly good, possibly, as they said, because no 'self-respecting germ would tolerate our living conditions'. A patrol was mostly routine and unspectacular, acting as air-sea rescue pickets for RAF and

USAAF bombers attacking targets on the mainland; sometimes, the excitement of landing and retrieving clandestine parties at remote beaches, when an error of judgement or identification by the Captain could lose not only the clandestine party but the whole submarine. The waters of the Malayan and Sumatran seaboards were studded with endless mazes of shoals, and hundreds of tiny offshore islands, some of them only a few feet above the water. In those confined shallows, a submarine had precious little sea-room or depth to evade a depth-charge attack. The sea was often glassy calm and a periscope stuck up like a sore thumb. Patches of sea-mist or tropical rain storms could easily conceal a target or an escort. Occasionally what appeared to be an island was really a target. The Japanese were masters of camouflage and some 'islands' covered with palms and foliage only betrayed themselves by their unusually rapid rate of change of bearing.

Targets were almost all tiny, hardly worth a torpedo, by Atlantic or Mediterranean standards. A ship of as much as 500 tons was cause for jubilation. One of 2,000 seemed a leviathan, as big as the *Queen Mary*. The Japanese pressed into service all manner of coastal craft. The usual targets were junks carrying twenty tons of rice, perhaps an armed trawler, a tug, or a schooner laden with coal or nickel ore, a small landing craft carrying fifty Japanese soldiers, a lighter with a thousand gallons of petrol, a tiny coaster with a cargo of foodstuffs, small fishing boats loaded with a catch for sale ashore, with some duck eggs, yams or fruit. Each in its minute way contributed to the Japanese war effort. Often passing fishermen would jeopardize a submarine by gaping and pointing and yelling at the periscope as it passed. The Chinese and Malay junk-masters and their crews, many of whom had been pressed into serving the Japanese, were surprisingly philosophical about the destruction of their junks, and sometimes even cooperative. But they did much prefer their junks to be sunk by gun-fire and not by demolition charges, so that they could gamble on the number of rounds required.

The enemy were not wholly toothless. On 21 November

Stratagem was sighted in the shallows of the Malacca Strait by an aircraft and then depth-charged by a destroyer and flooded. The Torpedo Officer and seven ratings escaped from the flooded submarine. Only the officer and two sailors survived captivity in Japan. On 16 January the veteran minelaying submarine *Porpoise* was overdue, probably sunk by Japanese aircraft. She was the 75th and last British submarine to be lost in World War Two.

[2]

THE EAST INDIES FLEET, 1945

HARD THOUGH THE EASTERN FLEET tried in 1944, all its efforts did not succeed in forcing the Japanese to divert any fresh resources into the area. The Japanese were too hard-pressed in the Pacific to spare any extra effort for the Indian Ocean. Many war correspondents noted and commented upon this. 'It could be said,' wrote A. W. MacWhinnie in *Illustrated* in February, 1945, 'that British naval strikes against the Japanese were of the tip and run variety, and that certain individual efforts amounted to little more than banging at the back door of the Japs and running away before the door was opened.'

That was cruel, but unfortunately true. However, the British Pacific Fleet was just about to change all that. That fleet had at last been formed after months of political in-fighting between the Prime Minister, the Foreign Office and the Admiralty and another long, and still incompletely resolved, internecine struggle between the Admiralty and the Ministry of War Transport. From the summer of 1944 onwards it had been common knowledge in the wardrooms and on the messdecks of the Eastern Fleet that the newest and fastest ships amongst them, with others coming out from UK every week, would form a new fleet to steam east and join the Americans in the Pacific. The great actions of the Pacific—Coral Sea, Midway, Guadalcanal, the Philippine Sea, and Leyte Gulf—had rumbled like distant thunder on the eastern horizon. Now, some of them would be going to join that great war.

Admiral Sir Bruce Fraser hoisted his flag as Commander in

Chief BPF in the battleship *Howe* on 22 November, 1944, and then flew to Sydney and on to Pearl Harbor to have discussions with Admiral Nimitz. He was followed later by his fleet, which sailed first on 17 December to carry out an aircraft strike on the oilfield at Pangkalanberandan in northern Sumatra, sailing again for a second attempt on 1 January, 1945. Finally the fleet sailed on 16 January for two major strikes against the important oil refineries at Palembang in southern Sumatra. The fleet, comprising four fleet carriers, the battleship *King George V*, four cruisers and ten destroyers, then sailed for Australia and, eventually, to join the American 5th Fleet off Okinawa in March, 1945.

Those who were left behind in Ceylon were inevitably left feeling rather flat. Commodore Evans-Lombe, Fraser's Chief of Staff, had been able virtually to pick and choose the officers he wanted. Fraser and Admiral Sir John Power, who had taken over as C-in-C East Indies Fleet, were old friends and fellow gunnery officers, and there were no hard feelings. But those who were not chosen obviously had slight feelings of being a 'Second Eleven'.

At its formation, the East Indies Fleet had some seventy ships, including escort vessels. They included the Third Battle Squadron (Vice-Admiral H. T. C. Walker, BS3) of the battleship *Queen Elizabeth* and the battle cruiser *Renown*, nine cruisers including the Dutch *Tromp* in the 5th Cruiser Squadron (Rear-Admiral A. D. Read, CS5), three escort and two ferry carriers under Rear-Admiral Clement Moody (Flag Officer Air) and eventually, some 24 destroyers. As more carriers arrived on the station, the 21st Aircraft Carrier Squadron was formed with Commodore G. N. Oliver (AC21) flying his broad pennant in the specially fitted aircraft direction cruiser *Royalist*.

In the first months of 1945 the East Indies Fleet's sense that they were in an operational backwater increased. In Ceylon the fleet was in the war, but not of it. One of the most beautiful islands in the world, Ceylon had experienced no warfare since the attack on Colombo harbour by Nagumo's aircraft on Easter Sunday, 1942. From the sea, the island was one of the most romantic sights in the east, rising from the horizon, like a blue wraith, like a mirage, with the smoky green crest of Adam's Peak above the bright green jungle which rolled right down to white beaches and the water's edge. On a calm day, when the sea lay like milky glass, the surface moved in mysterious ripples as though in phantom currents. Every morning the early watchkeepers could collect shining silvery flying fish from the fo'c'sles. Large whales lay submerged in the warm surface waters, basking in the heat of the sun. One submarine on surface passage rammed a whale with such an impact that she (the submarine) had to go into dry dock to repair her bows. The exotic smells, the spices and flowers, of Ceylon floated miles out to sea to welcome the sea traveller.

The Commander-in-Chief and the Flag Officer Ceylon had their headquarters in adjacent buildings at Colombo but the main base and fleet anchorage was at Trincomalee, a magnificent natural harbour in the north of the island. There, the main battle fleet lay in almost peacetime splendour in solid lines: first the battleships and the carriers, then the cruisers, and, on the fringes, the destroyers and frigates. The fleet normally kept tropical routine, starting work early, in the cool of the day, and securing for dinner in the early afternoon. For the sailors, there was the same time-honoured daily routine: scrub decks, gun drill, painting ship, cleaning during the long hot seemingly endless forenoons. With the sound of the bugles, the motor-boat engines as they passed from one ship to the next, the cries of native bumboatmen, Trincomalee had all the sounds of continuing imperial confidence. Under the awnings, the sun at midday reflected off the still water with an intensity that hurt the eyes. At noon there was the sailor's tot of rum, and an English cooked dinner of roast meat and veg. Then, in the afternoons, head down, and sleep.

Life at Trincomalee was summed up by five verses in the Fleet Poetry Broadsheet, published in August, 1945, at the Naval Headquarters, by a Lieutenant RN under the pseudonym of 'Lucy'.

Trincomalee

Dawnlight glows on the ships of the fleet again;
Sun beats new on the battle line.
Sleep sweaty sailors roused from their hammocks by
"Wakey, wakey, and rise and shine!"

"Scrub decks", "Gun drill", paint away and polish up
All through the long hot dull forenoon.
Faint not; fail not; wipe away that sweat again.
I smell sugar smell. Tots come soon!

Heads down, feet up, caulking all the afternoon,
Slumb'rous, snoring tropic routine.
Wait till the evening brings in the cool again;
Wait till the sun blaze leaves the scene;

Leave in the Dogs, so get into a Rickshaw;
Pad through the shack streets—God, the smell;
Rush to the sea's edge, and plunge in the cool green,
Float in the balm of the sea's slow swell.

Swiftly the night falls; black beneath the moonlight,
Palm trees sway in the monsoon gale.
Then to the Canteen, to knock back the one sole,
Weekly ration of luke-warm ale.

Memories of Ceylon are still vivid amongst the men of the fleet; the runny butter, and the tiny pigeon-size eggs, and the curious paw-paw jam. There were the flowers, tobacco flowers and stocks, and frangipani, and those with waxy petals strewn on the roadways, which nobody on the messdeck ever knew the name of. There were the shrines to Buddha and the little shops in Colombo selling dubious gem-stones and carved ivory; there were the roads crowded with dust-raising lorries and the bullock carts, all festooned about with hanging earthenware pots; there were the muddy water buffaloes in the paddy fields, and the great crows croaking on the rooftops, and the pale lizards crouching in corners, and the native villages, smelling of raw arrack spirit, and sweat and excrement and dried fish; there was the coming of Gracie Fields aboard, and the visiting ENSA performances, with their disquieting joking references to civilian hardships—not mentioned in the letters from home. There was swimming in the sea, with every now and again the sharp jab in the stomach and boom of the small anti-saboteur-swimmer charges they detonated each time the harbour entrance was opened. There were the sand crabs on the beach who vanished in a flurry of movement until they left only two eyes on stalks, like wary periscopes. There were soldiers in the mess, just passing through, with stories of Burma, and its trees and its rain, both of which went on for ever. There were open-air cinemas with performances for a thousand men under the tropical stars. Some of the ship's companies, especially the submarine crews, went to rest camps in the hills such as Diyatawala, 6,000 feet up. There was one air letter form a week, pretty thin for the married men, and the micro-film air letters: one sheet of paper photographed and made one frame of film. There were 'pep' talks from Lord Mountbatten the Supreme Commander, concerned that the fleet, like Slim's 14th Army in Burma, might come to think of themselves as 'forgotten'. There were salt tablets, and Mepacrin pills for malaria: to catch the disease was a punishable offence. Once again, a poet has caught the authentic atmosphere. Petty Officer Charles Causley was there in the light fleet carrier *Glory* later in the year:

Trincomali, ah, Trincomali!
The Technicolour market, the monkeys and chickens,
The painted boats at Vegetable Jetty,
The rattling lizard and the bored crow
In the burning graveyard:

25

Here lies David Kelly, Naval Stores Officer,
Died of the Fever,
1816.

O the drums and the pythons and the trick of the mango tree,
The warrior Buddha with the brandished sword,
The rosewood elephants and the porcupine cigarette boxes.
O the fire opal, zircon and water sapphire,
And the warm beer and peanuts in the P.O.s' canteen.
The Chinese cafés, and the rickshaw boys
Grinning and gambling by the fish-market.
The rings from Kandy and the black ivory elephants
Crossing the eternal bridge for the mantelshelves
Of thousands and thousands of sailors.

To go east from Ceylon, to advance physically and metaphoric-
ally towards the Rising Sun, was literally to go from peace to war,
although apart from the clandestine parties of Force 136, some
aircrew and submarine captains, very few men of the fleet had
ever seen the coastlines of Thailand, Malaya and Sumatra which
had been enemy-held for more than three years. By the beginning
of 1945, events had forced the Japanese Navy to reorganize their
depleted resources in the South-West Pacific and the Indian
Ocean. The South-West Pacific Fleet was restricted (first by
Allied pressure, now by Japanese decree) to the area immediately
around the Philippines. A new fleet, the 10th Area Fleet, was
created for the rest of the South-West Pacific which included the
Indian Ocean. The new C-in-C was Vice-Admiral Shigeru
Fukudome, who had commanded the now-disbanded Second Air
Fleet in the Philippines, with his naval headquarters at Singapore.
Many of the imposingly named naval forces the Japanese now
redeployed were forces in not much more than their imposing
names. The main operational fleet unit was the Second (there was
no First) Diversionary Attack Force. This may well have been
capable of carrying out a diversion, but certainly made no

attacks. It consisted primarily of the two converted hybrid battleship/carriers *Ise* and *Hyuga*, and the two heavy cruisers *Ashigara* and *Haguro*, forming the 5th Cruiser Squadron. Two more heavy cruisers, *Takao* and *Myoko*, were also at the Singapore naval base, where both had taken refuge after suffering severe damage in the Battle of Leyte Gulf. *Myoko* was repaired sufficiently to be able to make one attempt to return to Japan in December, 1944, but was torpedoed by the US submarine *Bergol* on the 13th and returned to Singapore. There she stayed for the rest of the war.

Takao also never moved again. She was still afloat, acting virtually as a floating gun battery overlooking the Johore Strait, when she was attacked and mined, and even more badly damaged, by the midget submarine *XE-3* in July, 1945. Another cruiser, *Oyodo*, operated with the 10th Area Fleet from 5 to 20 February, and a fourth, *Izudzu*, joined on 25 March, but lasted barely a fortnight before being sunk on 7 April in a co-ordinated attack by the US submarines *Charr*, *Gabilan* and *Besugo*, with peripheral assistance from the British submarine *Spark*.

Ise and *Hyuga* were recalled to Japan in February and sailed from Singapore on the 10th, loaded with aviation spirit and other precious war materials. With such valuable ships and cargoes at stake, the Japanese took great care to safeguard the two ships' passage, while the Allies, forewarned by Intelligence, made equally strenuous attempts to intercept them. With a combination of very good luck and very bad weather, both ships evaded numerous attacks by air and submarine and reached Moji in Japan on the 19th.

The 10th Area Fleet also included the 13th Air Fleet which also was only a fleet in name. Nominally it had two air flotillas, the 23rd and 28th, but by January, 1945, these had been whittled down to a few airfield units only, and one air group, the 381st, with the remnants of four other air groups attached. Even so, the remaining strength of about fifty fighters, five night-fighters and seventeen carrier torpedo-bombers might have made the difference

27

between life and death for many of *Haguro*'s ship's company, had the Imperial Japanese Navy and Army resolved their traditional mutual animosities and given the ship proper air cover.

By February, 1945, the Japanese empire in the East Indies was already crumbling at the edges to such an extent that Japanese garrisons were being withdrawn from outlying islands in the Moluccas, from Timor, the Lesser Sunda Islands and from dozens of scattered islands in the Panda and Arafura Seas. The Japanese intended to hold Java, Borneo and Sumatra as long as possible but to mount their main defence in Malaya and Indo-China. On 7 February the 10th Area Fleet was placed under the command of Field-Marshal Count Terauchi, C-in-C Southern Army Area, with his headquarters at Saigon. Count Terauchi planned to withdraw his outlying forces and to concentrate them in Malaya and Indo-China in four major evacuation programmes. They were designated SHO (Akiraka), the evacuation of troops from the Andaman and Nicobar Islands to Singapore; CHI, the movement of troops from Singapore to Indo-China, via Saigon; Transportation Plan No 10, which was the transfer of about 5,000 troops of the 48th Army Division from Timor to Singapore; and HO, the movement of troops from Borneo to Surabaya (although no details emerged of HO, and it seems it was probably never undertaken). The two heavy cruisers *Ashigara* and *Haguro*, with one old destroyer *Kamikaze*, were the only sizeable warships operational in the 10th Area Fleet capable of assisting and protecting these Japanese troop movements.

Here at last was a possible chance of action for the major surface ships of the East Indies Fleet. In 1945 the fleet's tasks were as numerous and complex as ever: to deny the Japanese the use of the Indian Ocean; to cut seaborne supply lines to the Japanese armies in Burma; to give close support on the seaward flank of 15th Corps in the new campaign in the Burmese Arakan which had opened in December, 1944; to attack Japanese shipping, oil and harbour installations. Since the summer of 1944 the Japanese had virtually abandoned the Indian Ocean, at least for the passage of large ships. Ceaseless attacks by Allied aircraft and submarines had forced them to use convoys of very small ships which crept inshore, hugging the land as close as possible. However, these evacuations and movements of Japanese troops might bring larger Japanese warships into the Indian Ocean. In February, 1945, the destroyers of the East Indies Fleet began a series of anti-shipping sweeps in the Andaman Sea, to look at whatever targets intelligence suggested or chance might bring up.

These destroyer sweeps were known as 'club runs' and the first of them (Operation SUFFICE) was carried out by Force 68, the 11th Destroyer Flotilla led by Captain H. Biggs (D.11) in *Rotherham*, with *Roebuck*, *Rapid* and *Rocket*, who left Trincomalee on 21 February. Force 68 met no enemy shipping, but *Roebuck* and *Rapid* carried out a short bombardment of Great Coco Island just after midday on the 24th. They broke off for an aircraft alarm but all four destroyers returned an hour later for a bombardment which lasted 45 minutes and which Captain Biggs conceded was carried out with more enthusiasm than effect. Some 990 rounds of HE, and seventeen of star-shell were expended, to damage one hut severely and slightly damage another, and possibly to destroy radar installations.

Captain Biggs' ships went to Akyab to refuel on 25 February and sailed again for another 'club run' (Operation TRAINING) on the 27th. This time they had more luck. They met an enemy convoy of three small coasters between Tavoy Island and Heinze Basin on the night of 1/2 March and sank all three by gunfire. On the 3rd Force 68 went to Port Blair in the Andamans and bombarded the harbour, sinking two sailing junks and damaging another three. There was some fire from shore batteries which the destroyer returned, and everybody in the flotilla was greatly encouraged by one large explosion ashore, which might have been a magazine detonating.

It had not been much of a 'club run' but at least it was a start. Captain Biggs admitted the results were meagre, but the sweeps had high training value. They had shown that the Japanese look-out and enemy reporting organization was poor. The Japanese seemed not to have enough aircraft to keep air control over the area and their shore-based radar systems were almost ineffective. The area, he said, was 'ripe for development'.

The next 'developers' were Force 70, led by Captain Manley Power in *Saumarez*, with *Volage* and *Rapid*. *Saumarez* had only arrived at Trincomalee on 10 March, having escorted the carrier *Formidable* bound for the British Pacific Fleet, from Alexandria. Power and his ship's company had only a few days to refuel and re-store, brief themselves on their new fleet-mates, and make their numbers with the C-in-C before sailing for Operation TRANSPORT on the 14th. It was Captain Power's first venture with the EIF and the experience turned out to be painful.

The 'club run' began almost eerily devoid of incident. Force 70 swept east towards Penang uneventfully. An intended reconnaissance of Langkawi Sound was abandoned because Japanese air activity had been reported. On the evening of the 17th the ships bombarded the railway works at Sigli, in Sumatra. Again there was no opposition, no sign of life at all, except as Captain Power reported, 'Smoke from a train and an enormous flock of white birds which withdrew in an orderly manner to the southward'.

Force 70 retired under cover of a rain squall and next day arrived off Great Nicobar. They spent most of the day steaming up and down examining the bays and inlets of the island, looking for targets. The weather had cleared, the sky was blue, the wind was a fresh, scented breeze, the hot sun beat down on an emerald sea and on beaches dazzlingly white, with bunches of cool palms. Like a holiday brochure, it all looked most inviting, but there was nothing to shoot at.

All this peaceful cruising engendered, as Captain Power said, a false sense of security. On the 19th Force 70's idyll was rudely shattered by the enemy. The ships closed Port Blair harbour at first light, but found no targets. By midday they were off the eastern end of Stewart Sound, a narrow stretch of water, opening from the south-east of the Andaman Islands, running between

North and Middle Island. The Sound ran roughly in the shape of a large figure J, with a peninsula guarding the entrance. Kwantung Point, a prominent feature on the peninsula, was known to be held by the Japanese and possibly defended by a battery of guns up to about six-inch calibre. The latest intelligence available to Captain Power was that only high-angle guns were in place, and when last seen the emplacements appeared derelict. (When Captain Power returned to Trincomalee, an Intelligence officer on the staff told him that they had actually been considering deleting all reference to Japanese defences in Stewart Sound when Power's first action report arrived.)

Shortly after 1.15 pm that afternoon *Saumarez* entered the Sound cautiously and alone. *Volage*, who was then steaming on one shaft, having had main condenser trouble and shut down one main turbine, was ready to fire air bursts over the suspected positions of the shore batteries if they were troublesome, while *Rapid* was ready to engage with direct counter-battery fire if necessary. The channel was so narrow at one point that the men on *Saumarez'* upper deck could hear the roar of the ship's boiler-room exhaust fans echoing off the jungle which came down like a green wall to the very water's edge, only a bare fifty yards away.

Just inside the entrance (at about 1.25 pm) *Saumarez* turned to port into a small bay. As the bay opened out, some uniformed men or perhaps natives, anyway the figures of men, were seen running towards a clearing in the trees. *Saumarez'* midships Bofors gun's crew were the first to see them and indicated the target in the quickest and most unambiguous manner by hosing them down with Bofors tracer shells. 'A' and 'B' 4·7 inch guns also opened fire, and *Volage* fired from outside the Sound, with air bursts over the clearing. But there was no more movement or any other response. The gun-site, if indeed it was a gun-site, was deserted and, as intelligence had reported, probably derelict.

Saumarez soon passed further into the channel, where her guns would no longer bear on the clearing, and was turning to port at 10 knots inside the bay when a small pier was sighted at the base of Kwantung Point with a junk alongside it. Captain Power ordered the Bofors to engage the target and ordered full astern to take way off the ship, at the same time putting his helm over to swing the stern and allow the after guns to bear. They were not needed. The second salvo from 'A' gun hit the junk squarely and demolished it in one leaping explosion of water.

Captain Power had ordered *Volage* and *Rapid* to join him in the Sound when the rumble of heavy gunfire was heard from the eastern entrance. At 1.50 pm a plaintive signal was received from *Volage*: 'Somebody is firing at us'. *Saumarez* went full astern to clear a projecting point of land, swung round, and returned the way she had come, working up to 24 knots as she approached Aves Island, in the middle of the channel. Rounding the island, Captain Power came upon an unpleasant sight.

Rapid was stopped, apparently dead in the water, lying broadside on to the channel. A large fire was burning amidships, plumes of steam were roaring from her funnels with a great deal of smoke and steam from her port side. She had dropped smoke floats to try and give herself some protection and, behind their straggling cover, *Rapid*'s guns were still firing at the clearing *Saumarez* had engaged on her way in. She was less than two thousand yards from shore, at almost point blank range for the Japanese gunners. Already great yellow shell splashes of near-misses were towering up on either side of her.

The Japanese had held their fire until *Saumarez* had passed into the Sound and until *Volage* and *Rapid* were at less than 2,000 yards range. Now they had *Rapid* almost at their mercy, a sitting target. She was hit four times within a few minutes, and suffered damage to both her boiler rooms. Both boiler rooms were evacuated, the ship lost power and came to a stop. Power now signalled to *Volage*: 'I will take *Rapid* in tow. Cover me with smoke.' *Saumarez* steamed in towards *Rapid*, firing at the gun which was battering *Rapid*. As *Saumarez* came alongside *Rapid*'s disengaged starboard side, bow to stern, shielding her own machinery spaces from the enemy guns with *Rapid*'s hull, *Volage* crossed ahead, laying a smoke screen with funnels and floats trying to draw the enemy's attention to herself.

Power's force was now in a very serious situation, in which all three ships could well be lost. They were all in a confined waterway, which was commanded by an enemy six-inch battery firing at very close range. *Rapid* was unable to move, and *Volage* in any case only had one shaft. *Saumarez* herself was temporarily attached to *Rapid* and was herself unable to manœuvre. There was worse to come.

A fifth shell hit *Rapid*'s 'X' mounting and killed or badly wounded almost all the gun's crew. Her midships 20 mm pompom was also out of action, and for the first time *Rapid*'s fire began to falter under the punishment. *Saumarez*' own fire was masked by *Rapid* and some of her guns' crews scrambled over the guardrails to man *Rapid*'s guns. The action duty of Lieutenant Denis Calnan, the Captain's Secretary, was to control the close range weapons. He normally had the massive weight of the remote-control spotting box strapped to his shoulders but had discarded it and scrambled across with the rest of his gun's crew:

'I had hardly looked at *Rapid* until that moment—I had been fully occupied in trying to get my tracers on the enemy battery—and I was unprepared for the bloody shambles I stumbled into . . .

'The pompom's crew were dead or dying. Eight bodies were hung around the mounting and the wounded lay in a bloody heap on the iron deck. There was a human lung draped over the gunsight, and half a man sitting in the trainer's seat. My orders were to get the gun into action again, so we bundled the dead men over the side as best we could. The whole corpses were easy enough to manhandle, but my heart failed me when I took a body by the shoulders and the upper half of the torso came away in my hands. But worst of all was the removal of the hunks of raw meat from the jagged steel around the gun—bare hands for this job, just like the local butcher in the village shop. Our green uniforms soaked and sticky with black blood, we then turned to the gun; but it was useless—solid, and two barrels split by splinters.

33

Meanwhile the wounded were being taken care of by the first aid parties, so back we clambered to our ship, bloody, sweaty and shaken.'

Saumarez' first aid parties were also shaken by what they saw. None of them had had first-hand experience of such a bloody carnage. One of them, Leading Steward Kenneth Marshall, said he was far more scared when *Rapid* was hit than by anything that happened in the action against *Haguro*.

Saumarez had all lines secured to *Rapid* only eight minutes after coming alongside and by 2.20 pm was working away towards the seaward entrance. *Rapid's* own screws were turning again astern and both were making about six knots. Meanwhile *Volage* was still making smoke and engaging the battery. As the other two ships were obscured in smoke *Volage* herself was now the enemy's only clear target and she herself was hit three times. At 2.39 pm she reported that she was hit and stopped. This, as Captain Power said with admirable under-statement, 'was an unpleasant moment, giving an unattractive prospect of two ships unable to steam and within the enemy range.' *Volage* had been hit by three shells (actually 155 mm calibre) only one of which, landing on 'B' gundeck and damaging the wheelhouse, caused most of the casualties of three killed and eight wounded. Of the other two, one failed to explode and the other hit the Wardroom wine store, destroying 26 bottles of stout. The hit on the wheelhouse put *Volage's* steering temporarily out of action and in the interval before emergency steering could be connected *Volage* careered close to *Saumarez* so that her wash parted two of the towing wires as she passed. Captain Power, with all manner of problems on all sides, signalled her to 'get the hell out of it'.

Volage followed *Saumarez* and *Rapid*, firing astern at the now silenced enemy battery, while working parties from both ships cleared the upper deck and evacuated seven of the most badly wounded to *Saumarez*. There, Surgeon Lieutenant A. M. Evans RNVR converted a seaman's messdeck into a temporary operating theatre. Working with only a towel round his waist and brief pauses for coffee, he laboured for twenty-four hours to save the lives of all seven. He was rightly awarded a DSC for his devotion to duty.

By 4 pm *Rapid*'s engine-room staff had managed to raise steam and connect one boiler and the ship was able to make 18 knots unaided. Her casualties had been heavy in spite of all Evans' efforts: one officer and ten ratings killed, two officers and 21 men wounded.

Force 70 reached Akyab on 20 March where battle damage was patched up with the help of the engine-room and shipwright department of the cruiser *Suffolk* who worked day and night to make, amongst other things, a complete plywood starboard side for *Volage*'s wardroom. *Rapid* later sailed to Simonstown for permanent repairs.

All in all, the action in Stewart Sound had been a chastening experience for everybody concerned. Cruising round these romantic-looking islands was not such a peaceful pursuit after all, nor were the Japanese as harmless as they sometimes appeared. Power and his fellow captains discussed the action in detail among themselves. Plainly, it was an error in Intelligence which had led to the débâcle. But this had been compounded, as Power admitted, by a degree of over-confidence. Memories of that afternoon, the green claustrophobic confines of that narrow Sound, the shell-fire, the bloody shambles on *Rapid*'s iron deck, would not quickly go away.

Meanwhile, the Japanese alarmed and puzzled Allied Intelligence by immediately broadcasting accurate details of the action, giving the names of *Saumarez* and *Volage*. The solution was not discovered until the end of April when a party of Japanese troops, equipped with radio, was flushed out of hiding on Baronga Island, south of Akyab. They had been there since Akyab was captured in January and had been spotting ship movements in the anchorage and intercepting signals between ships.

Largely thanks to *Suffolk*, *Volage* was fit for battle and sailed from Akyab as part of a reconstituted, reinforced and somewhat vengeful Force 70 on 25 March. Two more destroyers of the 26th Flotilla, *Virago* and *Vigilant*, had left Trincomalee when news of the Stewart Sound action arrived and now joined *Saumarez*. So, incidentally, the flotilla which was eventually to sink *Haguro* had already begun to assemble.

As Calnan's assistant, Writer Alan Parsons, later said, 'We seemed to find something nasty each time we left harbour.' And so it was again, although having led his ships out of a situation which might have been a tragedy, Captain Power was now to lead into an episode which also had the elements of an embarrassing comedy.

Saumarez had a 'Y' Party of RAF personnel who were all trained Japanese interpreters embarked, whose duty it was to monitor Japanese radio broadcasts and to aid the command in assessing enemy intentions. Although their work was not much discussed on board, it was nevertheless vital. They were often able to detect Japanese vessels in the vicinity and it was due to them, and to ULTRA intercepts which were available at Akyab before sailing, rather than to luck or coincidence, that when Force 70 entered the Andaman Sea through the North Preparis Channel on the morning of 26 March, a radar contact was detected at 10.30, range 21,000 yards. Force 70 formed line ahead and increased speed to close the target, which was sighted some fifteen minutes later.

The target was the nearest of a convoy of four small Japanese ships, bound from Singapore to Port Blair. They were the 1,500 ton *Rishio* Maru, with a cargo of rice, 130 men of a naval battalion (including a relief guns crew for Kwantung Point battery) and 18 women for the entertainment of the garrison; the 400 ton *Teshio* Maru, carrying food, general supplies, equipment, and sekkyu oil; escorted by two submarine chasers, Nos *34* and *63*.

Bearing in mind that in an E-boat action in home waters a British destroyer had once been disabled by the close-range weapons of her much smaller opponent, Captain Power decided to make his attack out of range of the Submarine Chasers' close-range weapons. *Saumarez* opened fire with 4·7 inch main armament at 10.59, range 14,000 yards, taking the nearer *Teshio* Maru as target. The other three destroyers, following behind their leader, opened fire as they came into range.

The convoy had turned to the south-west as soon as they sighted the destroyers. The two submarine chasers, though outgunned and outnumbered by larger and faster opponents, were small, elusive and highly manœuvrable, and were both handled with great dash and bravery, in the best traditions of the Imperial Japanese Navy. They first laid smoke screens to protect their charges and then returned through the smoke again and again to come within the destroyers' range, hoping to draw them away from the two merchant ships.

At this they were at first only too successful. Power and his fellow captains found the submarine chasers the most infuriating targets. After half an hour's furious firing, Force 70 had expended a prodigious amount of ammunition for no visible result. *Volage* had also fired four torpedoes at *Rishio* Maru, which she believed to be stopped—thus neglecting a basic rule of torpedo attack; a target very rarely has no way on at all. In fact *Rishio* Maru was still under way and the four torpedoes, each carefully aimed and fired at a range of 2,000 yards, all missed.

Saumarez had meanwhile made radio contact with two groups of patrolling RAF Liberators. The Liberator pilots were at first extremely suspicious of Force 70's English. The first two reported that they were armed only with depth-charges, and nothing more was heard from them. The second pair, evidently more impressed by Captain Power's command of the language, flew down almost to sea level to carry out their attack. Power noticed that, 'They were obviously intent on their fun. I had to pull my ships clear to make sure we did not get bombed.'

The leading Liberator approached *Rishio* Maru at about masthead height and dropped a stick of eight bombs, one of which hit *Rishio* Maru amidships. She blew up at once and sank in a few minutes. But, before the horrified eyes of the watching men in the destroyers, the Liberator's port wing tip appeared to strike the ship's mainmast and the great bomber spun cartwheeling over into the sea.

Saumarez closed the spot where the Liberator had disappeared, and picked up two survivors, Sergeants R. G. Radford and P. Roberts, RAF, both injured but thankful to be still alive and rescued. Meanwhile the rest of Force 70 had worked round to the south of the convoy. All were now very low in ammunition, except *Virago* who had been later into action. In *Volage*, Commander Durlacher later admitted in his report that 'he was appalled by the speed with which the ammunition disappeared. I had not realized how easy it was to get rid of some 900 rounds in a short space of time.' Everybody was therefore very relieved when eventually *Teshio* Maru succumbed to *Volage*'s gunfire. *Vigilant* sank one of the submarine chasers with one torpedo from a salvo of eight. Midshipman Walter Godsal, at his action station in the AA Director in *Volage*, had a grandstand view: 'It was as though the whole of the forepart was blown out of the water and folded backwards over the bridge. The ship disappeared in a matter of seconds.' The second submarine chaser was also sunk, by gunfire from *Vigilant* and *Virago*. And so at last, the whole convoy of four ships had been destroyed, after the expenditure of 18 torpedoes, 3,160 rounds of 4·7 inch ammunition, and a considerable amount of Bofors 40 mm ammunition. It had been, in Captain Power's phrase, 'an exasperatingly unsatisfactory action'—an opinion with which the Admiralty later fully concurred.

There were still the Japanese survivors in the water. *Saumarez* lowered scrambling nets over the side and approached them. They were mostly in one large group, with some stragglers. About twenty were retrieved uneventfully, but most of them, a party of more than thirty, provided the kind of diversion which the men of the fleet were coming to expect of Japanese survivors. Some just swam away from rescue. Others cut their own throats as the possibility of rescue approached them. One of them maintained the offensive Samurai spirit to the end, although he met his match in the Captain's Secretary, who many years later could still recall the scene vividly: 'I was standing abreast the torpedo tubes directing the rescue when I heard and felt a clang on the ship's side. There directly beneath me was a Japanese, heavily built and with a bald head. Half out of the water with one hand gripping the rescue net with the other he was hammering at the thin plate of our ship's side with the nose of what looked like an oerlikon shell. Instinctively I drew my pistol and, leaning far over the beading with one arm round a guard rail stanchion, jammed the barrel hard down on top of his skull. I could not think of anything else to do—I spoke no Japanese. Blood streaming down his face, he looked up at me, the pistol six inches from his eyes, the shell in his hand. I suppose I should have shot him—but I knew my gun was unloaded, which was more than he did. I do not know how long I hung in this ridiculous position eyeball to eyeball with a fanatical enemy, but it seemed too long at the time. At last he dropped the shell into the sea, brought up his feet, pushed off from the ship's side like an Olympic swimmer, turned on his face and swam away.'

Volage also suffered the same 'small-time, do-it-yourself kamikaze attack', in Midshipman Godsal's words, by another swimmer who was shot by an armed sentry on deck, thus getting the death he sought. In *Saumarez* Power had been getting impatient. It was never healthy to remain stopped at sea in wartime. The order was passed: 'No more prisoners, recover scrambling nets'. But for the indefatigable Captain's Secretary the day's events were not yet over:

'I moved forward to get out of the way of the net party when I saw a long slender arm—a girl's arm—wave from a mass of oil about thirty yards off our boom. The nets were inboard, the ship gathering sternway, but I did not stop to think—my action was instinctive and automatic—I whipped off my shirt and dived over the side. The water was delicious. As my head broke surface I came quickly to my senses, particularly because I saw and heard my Captain bellowing at me from the wing of the bridge, "Come back, you bloody young fool!" But by this time I was committed and thought I might as well enjoy my swim and rescue the girl too. I rescued the girl all right, but did not enjoy the swim. It did not take long to reach her, but for the last ten yards I had to swim through thick oil. Then I grabbed her shoulders from behind. Panic-stricken, she turned like a greased eel and had me in a vice, arms locked around my neck, fingernails deep into my back, teeth meeting in my cheek and legs wrapped around my hips. She was as naked as she was born. I fought her for my life. Gripping her hair with both hands I nearly broke her neck, pulling her head back until her face was under water. Then she went limp, and with nearly the last of my strength I swam her back towards the ship—by now fifty yards away.

'My reception on board was mixed. Cheering sailors making unprintably coarse comments, an angry Captain—but I was glad enough just to be back on a familiar deck—and to hell with being a hero. Never again, I swore as the oil fuel began to burn my eyes and cheek and the deep scores across my back.'

Five naval officers, forty-one men and seven women were rescued by *Saumarez* and *Volage*. The men were naval ratings, crews of the merchant ships, and some assorted passengers. The women, according to Lt-Commander Tyers, *Saumarez*'s First Lieutenant, were 'mostly third class prostitutes for the Japanese troops on the islands'. One of them, 'Mary', was heavily pregnant and another appeared to have suffered a miscarriage while being rescued. A half-caste girl, 'Chatya', knew scraps of English, including 'Kiss me, darling' and snatches of popular songs; according to the other survivors she was 'Joro', an 'entertainment girl'. The women were taken under the care of 'Doctor' Evans who gave them tranquillisers—much to their horror, as they thought they were being injected with poison.

In *Volage* the prisoners were seated on the upper deck. As they recovered one of them jumped over the side. The sentries could do very little to prevent him: to shoot him would be to give him what he most desired. However, most of the prisoners in *Saumarez* and *Volage* accepted their fate philosophically, eventually forming a 'dhoby' party to do the ship's laundering. But when *Volage* entered Trincomalee on 28 March, another Japanese was found to have hanged himself with his loincloth in the Chief and PO's bathroom. When the pinnace came alongside to take the prisoners off to captivity on Sober Island the body of the dead shipmate was surreptitiously lowered into the boat and dispatched with the rest.

The prolonged gunfire had reduced *Volage*'s makeshift wardroom bulkhead to matchwood once more. *Volage* was sent to Durban to refit and dropped out of the 26th Flotilla's story.

The destruction of that convoy deprived the Andaman garrison not only of their 'Joros' (of whom 21 had originally taken passage) but also of desperately needed food. By July, 1945, the food shortage in the islands was serious and the Japanese committed several atrocities on the civilian population. Three hundred 'useless mouths' i.e. the aged and infirm, women and children, and all those who were not employed by the Japanese and therefore had no ration cards, were taken from their houses, stripped of their possessions and embarked on three ships. Off Havelock Island, a jungle-covered uninhabited island off the north-east coast of South Andaman, the Japanese forced many of these people into the water, to wade ashore. By 21 September, 1945, only eleven were still alive. Allied investigators found the bones and skulls of a hundred and eight men, women and children on the island and the remains of many others in the sand below highwater mark.

On 13 August, some seven hundred more men, women and children were taken to the island of Taimugli where they were all shot by a firing party of nineteen Japanese soldiers. The bodies were thrown into mass graves and covered with earth. However, the officer in charge was ordered by Army headquarters in the Andamans to return to the island, exhume the bodies and burn them. If asked, he was to say that they had all been taken safely

41

to Port Campbell and released. It was this sort of behaviour, combined with reports, already general knowledge in the fleet, of the treatment of Allied prisoners of war and civilian internees, which aroused such an unusual tide of hatred against anything Japanese.

The month of April was a busy one for the fleet, beginning with another 'club run' by the 11th Destroyer Flotilla along the Tenasserim coast between Mergui and Amherst (Operation PENZANCE). Force 62, *Rotherham* (D.11), *Racehorse*, *Redoubt* and *Rocket*, reconnoitred Narcondam Island on the morning of 1 April, to judge its suitability as a fuel and ammunition dump for coastal forces (it was thought not suitable) and then sank their first targets, a small auxiliary coaster and a junk, in a night encounter in the early hours of 2 April. On the 4th they bombarded the luckless radar station on Great Coco Island and returned to Akyab the next day to refuel. Two days later they sailed again for a sweep of the coast of Burma between Mergui and the Moulmein River (Operation PASSBOOK), sinking seven junks and assorted sailing craft between 9 and 11 April.

Early on the 11th Liberators of 222 Group RAF pulled off a notable *coup* by bombing and sinking the Japanese net-tender *Agata* Maru and her escort, Submarine Chaser No 7, north-east of the Nicobars. Force 62 closed the scene of the sinkings that afternoon and, despite suicides and sharks, picked up the unusually large number of sixty-two Japanese survivors, and six very young Sumatran boys wearing Japanese uniforms.

Telegraphist Robert Sandford, in *Rotherham*, was one of those horrified by the behaviour of some Japanese survivors. 'When we arrived at the position [of the sinking] many Japanese were in the shark-infested sea. We invited them to come on board, but they refused to do so although we could see the sharks taking limbs and some actually going under and being disposed of. Captain Biggs ordered seamen to retrieve about ten with boat-hooks which they did and as one was pulled on deck he promptly took out a knife and committed *hara-kiri*. When he died two minutes later Captain Biggs ordered a 4·7 inch cartridge case to be roped between his legs and he was just dumped over the side. We all felt sorry for this young man who later we found out was the skipper of the ship. One of our seamen was a bearded South African, a big man, and captain of the water polo team [a popular naval sport in Trinco harbour]. He dived into the sea and swam about 50 yards ignoring the sharks to rescue a brief case floating on the surface. On his return he was given a roasting by the Captain but I believe was decorated after the war. We brought the survivors back to Trinco, every ship cheering us in. Apparently we were the first to bring Jap prisoners in to Trinco.'

On 8 April, while Biggs's destroyers were still at sea, Vice-Admiral 'Hookey' Walker sailed from Trincomalee with a powerful Force 63 for a mixed programme of air strikes, anti-shipping sweeps, bombardments, and photo-reconnaissance flights over the Port Swettenham and Port Dickson areas (Operation SUNFISH). Admiral Walker's ships sailed in two groups: Group One, *Queen Elizabeth* (flag), the French battleship *Richelieu* (which had relieved *Renown* on 28 March), the cruiser *London*, with *Saumarez*, *Verulam* and *Vigilant*; and Group Two, the escort carriers *Emperor* (flag of Rear-Admiral W. R. Patterson who relieved Admiral Read as CS5 on 11 March) and *Khedive*, the cruiser *Cumberland*, with *Venus* and *Virago*.

Photo-reconnaissance had become one of the fleet's most important strategic tasks. On 3 February, 1945, Lord Mountbatten had received a fresh directive from the Combined Chiefs of Staff that, subject to successful liberation of Burma, the next main task in SEAC was the liberation of Malaya and the reopening of the Malacca Strait. For the landings at Port Swettenham and Port Dickson and the preparation for the advance south to Singapore (Operation ZIPPER), the staff planners would require up-to-date and detailed information on the Japanese resources and dispositions, harbours, airfields, and defences on the Malay peninsula and the coast of Sumatra. The planners were particularly interested in Phuket Island, at the north entrance to the Malacca

Strait, for which a seaborne landing was proposed (Operation ROGER), to provide an excellent forward naval, air and general supply base for the advance on Singapore. These areas were beyond the normal range of shore-based photo-reconnaissance aircraft and, although B-29s of the US 20th Bomber Command carried out a certain number of P.R. flights, the main task was done by aircraft of the fleet.

The first reconnaissances of the Kra Isthmus, Phuket, and northern Sumatra had actually been made by 888 Squadron Hellcats flying from *Ameer* at the end of February and the beginning of March in Operation STACEY. *Ameer* had sailed from Trincomalee under Admiral Walker, flying his flag in *Empress*, on 22 February, accompanied by the cruiser *Kenya*, with *Volage*, *Virago* and *Vigilant*, and the frigates *Spey*, *Swale* and *Plym*. The weather had been generally good for photography, with clear visibility, high cloud and light winds. But STACEY had not been without frustrations; there were camera failures on the first day, 26 February, and the light winds and temperamental catapults meant the carriers had to steam at high speeds to fly off their aircraft at all. These small, 11,400 ton *Ruler* Class escort carriers had a top speed of about 18 knots and normally carried about 24 aircraft. In hot weather, living conditions on board them were extremely trying. At high speeds temperatures in the machinery spaces regularly climbed to 140° or 150°, with very high humidities. The ships had little or no air-conditioning, even for tropically-sensitive radio and radar equipment. In the air direction room for instance, some 22 men were crushed into a small, airless compartment which had no scuttles leading to the open air, and no exhaust ventilation.

The Avenger bombers had their frustrations, too. One dropped 40,000 propaganda leaflets over the Kra Isthmus area on 28th, but two bombing strikes were cancelled because of lack of targets, and a third strike was abandoned because there were no maps or briefing material. But the fighters made up for the disappointment. The weather stayed clear, and though there was a bright moon approaching the full every night, the force was undetected until 1 March, just after 8 am, when Japanese aircraft attacked for the first time. 808 Squadron Hellcats from *Ameer* shot down a Dinah* and, two hours later, a flight of four Hellcats of 804 from *Empress* shot down an Oscar.* This was what the flight commander, Lieutenant John Myerscough RNVR, called 'a very, very accurate interception. We were put in an excellent position to attack from out of the sun. The enemy aircraft did not see us at all!' Shortly after dinner, *Ameer*'s Hellcats shot down another Oscar, to complete a very successful and heartening day. As everybody soon realized on board the carriers, these were the very first Japanese aircraft to be shot down by fighters from British escort carriers.

When Force 63 sailed for SUNFISH on 11 April, the first morning at sea was spent embarking air groups from the station ashore at China Bay. One Hellcat of 808 Squadron crashed into *Khedive*'s stern and burst into flames. The pilot was killed. Two days later another Hellcat of 808 Squadron missed all the arrester wires, crashed through the wire safety barrier and took another Hellcat with it on its flaming passage over the side. The pilot, a petty officer and two air mechanics were killed. 808 Squadron were new to the East Indies and this was a discouraging start for them.

Six specially fitted photo-reconnaissance Hellcats of 888 Squadron were embarked in *Emperor*. They had planned to start work on 12 April, but the flights had to be postponed for two days because of persistent catapult trouble. The surface bombardments were therefore brought forward to the 11th, when *Queen Elizabeth*, *Richelieu* and *London* bombarded Sabang, whilst *Saumarez*, *Vigilant* and *Verulam* went for Uleelhoe. There were no ship targets at Sabang, but the bombarding ships were attacked by a group of about ten Oscars just as they were withdrawing. 808 Squadron were able to make up for their dull start by shooting down an Oscar, and then, later in the afternoon, an

*Allied names for Japanese aircraft. Girls' names denoted bombers, boys' names fighters.

unwary Dinah. But an unidentified Japanese aircraft then surprised everybody by slipping out of cloud and dropping two bombs amongst the force, fortunately without causing any damage. Again and again, as at Stewart Sound and in a dozen other incidents, the Japanese showed this disconcerting habit of being able to strike back unexpectedly, apparently out of nowhere.

After fuelling from Force 70 (Royal Fleet Auxiliary [RFA] *Echodale*, escorted by the frigate *Lossie*) on 12 April, Force 63 closed the west coast of Sumatra and Photo-Reconnaissance (PR) flights were flown as planned, from a position west of Padang, on the 14th and 15th. The weather was very bad over Malaya on the 14th, the photographs were of poor quality, and to end a grim day, a very experienced PR pilot, Sub-Lieutenant J. W. Tomlinson RNVR, was lost when his Hellcat ditched in the sea ten miles off Port Swettenham.

Japanese aircraft were approaching at heights above 30,000 feet where the Hellcats, which were not fitted with long-range tanks, had to expend prodigious amounts of fuel and oxygen to climb up and get them. The Hellcats themselves, in one pilot's opinion, 'were becoming distinctly jaded', and at least one pilot on the 15th had to break off an interception above 30,000 feet because of lack of oxygen. However, one Oscar was shot down that day, and another was dispatched the following day, 16 April, during a strike on Emmahaven, the port of Padang, when a 400-ton merchant ship was also strafed and damaged. To set against that, yet another Japanese aircraft, an Oscar, penetrated to the Force on 15th and dropped two bombs. Neither did any damage, but Admiral Walker signalled a sharp reprimand to his ships, pointing out in the plainest terms that once again the enemy had escaped without being fired upon by a single ship.

By this late stage in the war, everybody in the fleet knew of the terrible way in which prisoners of war and civilian internees were being ill-treated, starved, beaten and denied medical supplies by the Japanese. The biblical text 'Love thine enemy' found no echo in any bluejacket of the East Indies Fleet. On the contrary, there was by now quite an unusual tide of personal hatred running against the Japanese which went far beyond any feeling against the Germans and Italians. Anything which might have any possible use for the Japanese, or anyone who might have any connection with them, was mercilessly attacked. This was well shown by an incident on 16 April. *Venus* and *Virago* had been detached from the Force at 5.30 that morning to carry out an anti-shipping sweep close in to the Sumatran shore. The only targets hardly justified the title of shipping, being a handful of small junks and fishing craft, of very doubtful value to the Japanese, hidden in the bays and behind the islands of Ayerbangis Bay, Temang Roads and Natal Roads. Nevertheless they were engaged and sunk by gunfire. As Commander Graham de Chair, in *Venus*, said, 'My instructions were to destroy all shipping on the coast of Sumatra but our activities and time were restricted to a small part of it and we only found junks hidden behind islands. These provided good target practise for the gunlayer of 'A' gun and some interesting pilotage for me. We had no wish to slaughter the crews of these junks, believed to be Sumatran fishermen, and generally fired a warning shot before opening fire. In one case the next round brought down the mast on a man's head as he was abandoning ship. We set fire to the junks as we passed or sank them. Admiral Walker called it butchery.'

Midshipman John Robathan, in *Venus*, like all the young, kept a bleak eye on the doings of his elders. He also kept a diary (illegally, in wartime) and recorded the events of 16th in it, detailing the numbers of junks sunk and the manner, and, he went on, 'Just before this, we did something which was far worse than heretofore: we opened up with 4·7 inch guns on a small canoe with three natives in it and it could not have been bigger than the canoe that brings the dhobeying in Trinco. Entirely defenceless and two miles away from the coast and not even a rock to chuck back at us: a senseless and childish thing to do, an act, which to my mind, disgraced the damn great "battle ensign" at our fore-peak.

'I cannot but think that those natives, probably Malays or Chinese, had rarely heard of the Japanese, and could not have been less interested as to what the big powers of the world were doing. Their livelihood probably lay in those fishing vessels and they cannot but feel a resentment against us for coming and removing it. It is lucky that we were not sunk and obliged to take refuge there, as we could not probably expect any help from those natives whose interests we disregarded. Also, it will be no easier for the Army if they invade, to find the natives already hostile to the British flag. It would have been much better to have acted as do our submarines. We could easily have lowered a motor boat and gone to each junk to investigate it and destroy it with demolition charges should there be any cause for it, instead of wasting valuable ammunition.'

Robathan's opinion was shared by Lieutenant John Gritten RNVR, who was on board *Venus* as a war correspondent at the time, writing for the *Times of Ceylon*. Many years later, when he was in Fleet Street, he still recalled the incident. 'To the incredulity and horror of, I am sure, many on board besides myself, the order was given to open fire on this canoe. To give the commander the benefit of the doubt, I do not know what his specific orders were in such a situation or how much discretion he was allowed. However, the 4·7 inch guns duly opened up and several rounds were fired. Each shell sent up a fountain of water, well wide of the canoe. *Venus* steamed on, the canoeists paddled for dear life. And I particularly noticed that *Virago* astern made no attempt either to fire or intercept the "enemy"—a tacit criticism, I thought, of our own action. A little later I was standing close to the for'ard guns crew among whom an argument was evidently going on. Above the hubbub came a Glaswegian voice—I suspected it was defiantly raised in the hopes that the words might carry as far as the bridge: "If we had hit those poor bastards, I'd never have looked my mother in the face again!".'

This admittedly unedifying episode shows the difficulty of distinguishing, in action, between neutral and enemy. *Pace*

Gritten's man on the forward gun, the prevailing mood in the fleet at that time was to destroy anything suspected of being Japanese first, and inquire later.

The behaviour of Japanese survivors continued to amaze and disgust the men of the fleet. On 29 April, Force 62, of *Roebuck*, flying the broad pennant of Commodore A. L. Poland, Commodore Destroyers, East Indies Fleet, with *Racehorse* and *Redoubt*, were on another 'club run' (Operation GABLE) patrolling the Gulf of Martaban. At fifteen minutes after midnight on 30 April a small junk was sighted from *Roebuck*, and several other junks were sighted soon afterwards. Starshell revealed a Japanese convoy of four small junks, seven larger junks, with a small escort vessel. The whole convoy was destroyed by gunfire. No survivors allowed themselves to be picked up at the time, but when Force 62 returned to the scene at first light, *Redoubt* rescued five Japanese. *Roebuck* approached a party of six Japanese clinging to the floating wreckage of a junk. One of them, it seemed, had a grenade and when the destroyer was quite close to them, he pulled out the pin. 'It was,' as Commodore Poland commented, 'an astonishing and rather unpleasant sight so soon after breakfast.'

The Japanese naval staff at Singapore were not so careless of lives as their men. This convoy, and the one so laboriously sunk by the 26th Destroyer Flotilla in March had both been lost without transmitting a distress message. As far as the Japanese knew, they had both vanished without trace. All ships were therefore ordered to exercise the sending of distress signals when under attack.

The convoy Commodore Poland's ships had destroyed was carrying some 750 Japanese troops from Rangoon to Moulmein. Unknown to, or at least unreported by, Allied Intelligence the Japanese had begun to evacuate the city on 23 April and these troops were almost the last to leave, the evacuation being completed by the 29th. Two days later the pilot of an aircraft flying over Rangoon saw the words 'Japs Gone! Exdigitate!' painted on the roof of Rangoon gaol.

For SEAC Rangoon had been for years like the end of the rainbow, like the Holy Grail, long sought after, always to be disappointed, over the next horizon, in sight but never in hand. Planning in SEAC throughout the war was in a constant flux of change and an assault on Rangoon (Operation DRACULA) was one of those undertakings which were always being put back because of events elsewhere: malaria amongst the troops, political unrest in India, shipping needs for TORCH and then for Salerno, landing craft requirements for Anzio, the failure of the bold thrust at Arnhem to end the war in Europe in 1944—all at various times vitally affected SEAC planning.

But, marvellously, by the early spring of 1945 the situation had changed. The campaign in the Arakan and General Slim's brilliant and subtle advance in central Burma were both going so well that the idea of DRACULA, perhaps in November, 1945, began to be discussed in cautious tones. Bearing in mind that the Americans had always made it clear that aid to China was more important to them than any British advance in Burma, Lord Mountbatten had two main courses of action for the spring and summer of 1945. He could abandon DRACULA and rely upon a rapid advance by Slim's 14th Army to take the city from the landward side before the monsoon came, and then undertake the assault on Phuket Island (Operation ROGER), to prepare the way for Singapore. Or he could abandon ROGER, allow for a slower advance by Slim, and mount an assault on Rangoon with reduced forces, a modified DRACULA, in fact.

Lord Mountbatten's commanders assured him on 23 February that the first choice was perfectly feasible, provided that enough air transport bases in Arakan were developed in time. The first plan was therefore chosen, to be followed by ROGER in June, the Port Swettenham and Port Dickson landings (ZIPPER) in October, and Singapore (MAILFIST) in December, 1945.

Hardly had this been decided, when, as usual in SEAC, it was all changed. The overland advance to Rangoon fell behind schedule. The Chinese demanded the return of their troops to

China. The Americans announced that from 1 June nearly half of the transport aircraft supplying 14th Army would be withdrawn. These events faced Lord Mountbatten with yet another difficult decision. The monsoon was due on or about 5 May. If 14th Army could not reach Rangoon and develop at least some of its port facilities by 1 June, then the army would have to retreat to some point where it could be supplied by land. This might even mean retreating to the Chindwin river, with a catastrophic effect on the war in South-east Asia and on the morale of 14th Army. To have come so far, to have endured so much and to have done so well, only to have to fall back for want of air transport would be too much. On 2 April Lord Mountbatten took the bold decision to postpone ROGER and mount a modified DRACULA, with one seaborne Division, the 26th Indian Infantry Division, and one airborne battalion, the 2nd Gurkha Parachute Battalion. D-Day for the assault was fixed for 2 May, 1945.

There were many special problems in an attack on Rangoon: there was the very short time left for planning; the lack of recent hydrographic information about the Rangoon river, where the Japanese had taken away most of the navigational aids, and the Allies had dropped many mines; the weather, which was not likely to be good, and would be much worse after the monsoon broke; the state of the tides, which meant that the assault convoys would have to arrive off Rangoon in darkness, and their strength, which restricted many landing craft movements to certain times. In spite of all the difficulties the main assault force sailed from Kyaukpyu in four convoys at roughly 24-hour intervals from 28 April. There were some breakdowns and leaking craft but the force arrived in good order and on time off the entrance to the Rangoon river. The moon was full but the whole operation was carried out under the almost unbroken gloom of a meteorological phenomenon which was actually known as the 'Dracula Depression', with frequent thunderstorms and heavy rain.

In the event, like many long-awaited parties, DRACULA was an anti-climax. The Japanese had gone. The Gurkhas were parachuted on to Elephant Point and took it after a brief skirmish. When the city was discovered to be free of Japanese, the DRACULA plan was modified, gunfire support plans and troop movements were changed, and the city reoccupied quietly, with no more fighting than when it had been lost more than three years earlier. The deserted streets were strewn with heaps of Japanese currency notes, now of only collector's interest. The shops were empty. There was no electric power, water supply or public sanitation service. Jetties and canals had fallen into disrepair. Since the Japanese left, there had been looting and arson. In the dockyard, machinery had been smashed, sheds bombed or looted, berths obstructed by wreckage or placed obstructions. There were only three berths for ships of moderate draught. Otherwise the great port was almost completely derelict. However, minesweeping and clearance began at once and on 6 May the landing ship *Glenroy*, drawing 29 feet, berthed alongside.

A few hours after the landing forces were put ashore on 2 May, the monsoon broke early and torrential rain fell all over the Burma battlefront. 4th Corps, which had been only a few miles north of Rangoon, entered the city on 3 May, unopposed.

Fighter cover over the Rangoon assault convoys was provided from 30 April by the 21st Aircraft Carrier Squadron, led by Commodore Oliver, flying his pennant in *Royalist*, with *Hunter*, *Stalker*, *Khedive* and *Emperor*, the fighter direction cruiser *Phoebe*, and escorted by *Saumarez*, *Venus*, *Virago* and *Vigilant*. Except for the loss of Sub-Lieutenant C. de G. Vyner RNVR, of *Hunter*, who was missing, presumed killed, after flying into the sea during a rain-squall on the morning of the 2nd, the 21st AC's part in DRACULA was almost uneventful. One 'bogey'* appeared on radar screens on the afternoon of 2 May but soon faded. *Virago* and *Khedive* collided slightly on completion of fuelling on 4th, the same day the ships were released from DRACULA.

Every available ship in the East Indies Fleet not actually involved in DRACULA took part in the covering operation (BISHOP)

*Unidentified radar contact.

in the Andaman Sea, to confuse the Japanese and to prevent any possible Japanese air or sea interference with the landings. *Haguro* and *Ashigara* were still in Singapore, and *Takao* was, just conceivably, seaworthy again. The Japanese might also try to stage reinforcement aircraft through the Andaman and Nicobar Island airfields. Nobody knew at that time, of course, that the successes of the 14th Army had already forced the Japanese to begin to evacuate Rangoon.

The submarines *Scythian*, *Statesman* and *Subtle* established patrol lines in the southern Malacca Strait, with *Strongbow* in the eastern Bay of Bengal and *Seadog* off the Tenasserim coast. RAF Sunderlands and Liberators, based on the Arakan coast, carried out cross-over patrols from the southern Andaman Islands eastwards to Tenasserim.

Force 63 for BISHOP sailed from Trincomalee on 27 April, with *Queen Elizabeth* (flag of Admiral Walker), *Richelieu*, *Cumberland* (CS5), *Suffolk*, *Ceylon*, *Tromp*, *Empress* (20 Hellcats of 804 Sq), *Shah* (10 Avengers of 851 Sq, 4 Hellcats of 804), *Rotherham* (D.11), *Tartar* (D.10), *Verulam*, *Nubian* and *Penn*. 'Hookey' Walker had a free hand to devise what operations he pleased. On the 30th, Force 63 carried out a dawn bombardment and Hellcat strike on both airfields at Car Nicobar, which were left cratered, harbour installations were destroyed, two 150 ton ships, five small vessels and a pier were also strafed and set on fire. Walker's ships then moved on to Port Blair that evening, strafing and cratering the airfield runways, bombarding the harbour and the town, and scoring two direct hits on Government House. For the next two days, the ships shuttled back and forth between the Andamans and the Nicobars, attacking Car Nicobar on the 1st and Port Blair on the 2nd.

On D-Day, 2 May, air reconnaissances were flown along the Burma coast between Heinze Basin and the Tavoy River. Two 80-ton coasters were bombed at Tavoy Point. At 3 pm that afternoon the fleet split into two groups. Force 64—*Queen Elizabeth*, *Tromp*, *Tartar* and *Penn*—went to fuel on 4 May while Force 68—

Cumberland, Richelieu, Ceylon, Rotherham, Roebuck and *Redoubt*, with the carriers—made armed air reconnaissances of shipping between Mergui and Victoria Point. Airfields at Victoria Point were strafed and grounded aircraft destroyed.

The two Forces kept a rendezvous on 5 May, Force 68 going to refuel, while Force 64 took up the strikes against shipping at Port Blair and Phoenix Bay, shooting up the radar and D/F station at Mount Harrier. On 6 May, the battleship *Queen Elizabeth* lay off Stewart Sound and with four crisp 15-inch shell hits cleaned out the gun positions on Kwantung Point which had caused Captain Power and his ships so much anguish on 19 March. Operations ended the next day with final air strikes by Hellcats on Car Nicobar.

Such was the command the Allies had now gained over sea and air in the Indian Ocean that during the twelve days of BISHOP Admiral Walker's ships met no opposition of any kind. One 'bogey' only was reported early on 1 May. However, the Japanese gunners were as alert and accurate as ever, given the chance. One of *Empress*'s Hellcats, piloted by Sub-Lieutenant J. A. Scott RNVR, was lost to flak over Port Blair on the morning of the 6th, the aircraft actually crashing into the sea within sight of the ship.

There was another incident at 5.20 pm that same day, which was an omen for the future. The 'Y' Party in *Venus* intercepted enemy radio transmissions bearing dead astern. The transmission carried the callsign of the Japanese heavy cruiser *Haguro* and suggested she might be following the force. *Hunter* flew off two Seafires which searched along the bearing for forty miles, without sighting anything. Later, the transmissions were found to be coming from Singapore. Meanwhile, as it was getting dark the two Seafires turned back and, when they landed on board it was quite dark. Both Seafires made heavy landings—understandably, since both pilots had forgotten to take off their sunglasses.

VE Day, Victory in Europe, was declared on 8 May, while the ships were on passage back to Trincomalee. While huge crowds gave themselves over to celebrations in London, Paris and New

York, all ships of the East Indies Fleet spliced the mainbrace and held services of thanksgiving. As they stood in their rows by divisions on the quarterdecks, bareheaded in the sunshine, many officers and men turned their thoughts from their wives and families at home to the future here in the East. All might now be quiet in the west but the Japanese Empire still cast a long and sinister shadow, still formidable, still menacing. It was still a long war and a hard war. On Okinawa the US Army and Marines were having to fight for every knob and knoll, blasting and burning the Japanese out of every cave and crack in the ground. The remains of the Japanese Navy lay immobilized in the harbours of metropolitan Japan, but at sea off Okinawa, the US Fifth Fleet and the British Pacific Fleet were being subjected to an almost daily wind of destruction, as squadrons of *kamikazes* dived out of the sky to immolate themselves on ships' decks and superstructures.

The men of the East Indies Fleet listened to Winston Churchill broadcasting to the nation and then later, during the Middle Watch by Ceylon time on the 9th, to HM the King. As Midshipman Robathan wrote 'all we could do was to think of home and wish we were there to join in the celebrations and hear the church bells'. By the afternoon of the 9th the whole fleet—two battleships, six escort carriers, five cruisers and thirteen destroyers—was back in harbour and began to refuel and rearm. Everybody was tired out by DRACULA and BISHOP. Apart from the depressing effect of the gloomy weather, anti-climax in war was often as exhausting as action. The ships had spent days altering course to fly off and land on aircraft, changing screen formations by day and night, exercising gun drills and routine action stations, waiting for attacks which never came. Nobody would have believed that a city of the stature of Rangoon could be taken without a savage reception from the Japanese.

At Trincomalee there were few facilities for celebrations but the men of the destroyer flotillas, spurred on by an extra tot to splice the mainbrace and an extra pint of Australian beer to mark VE Day, did their best. When the radio in the Fleet Canteen announced that celebratory bonfires were being lit at home, some men of the 26th Destroyer Flotilla shouted, 'There's a bonfire here!' and burned down part of the canteen and nearby *basha* huts. Meanwhile the 11th Flotilla had an unarmed combat with ratings from *Richelieu*. In *Cumberland* the celebrations included the throwing overboard of a mounted fragment of a French shell which had inflicted damage on the ship at Dakar in 1940. But for many of the fleet, it was a quiet evening on board, with a film on the fo'c'sle, reminiscences on the messdecks and in the wardroom. It was still a long war in the east, but just for this evening, there seemed to be time for a smoke and reflection.

At 10 pm that evening a general alarm was flashed around Trincomalee, ordering almost every ship there to raise steam and prepare to leave harbour at 6 am the next morning. In *Saumarez*, some of the sailors thought they were being sent to sea as punishment for burning down the canteen. But it was to be much more than that.

[3]

0600/10-2359/14 MAY, 1945
THE PRELIMINARY MOVES

'ALL SHIPS ADDRESSED . . .' the signal was classified Top Secret and priority Immediate, '. . . raise steam for 16 knots by 0600 10 May. Proceed in Groups to be signalled.' The main reaction of the men of the East Indies Fleet to that signal was a great communal groan of disappointment, mixed with apprehension. It was a sharply cruel reminder that, whatever might be happening in Europe, 'their war' out here was not over. The completion of DRACULA and the news of VE Day had inevitably caused a temporary lowering of their guard. They were all, in any case, very tired after twelve days' continuous operations. The ships were short of fuel, stores and ammunition. In wartime every ship returning to harbour began to refuel at once, as a matter of course. But the work of restoring and reammunitioning went on all night in some ships.

For 851 Squadron of Avenger torpedo-bombers, who were to play a crucial part in the operation to come, it was a particularly busy night. They were embarked in the escort carrier *Shah* but her accelerator was defective and later that evening the news arrived that the squadron aircraft would operate from *Emperor*. They would fly over to their new carrier on the first chance at sea. Meanwhile, squadron stores had to be transferred now. The night was spent packing stores and spare gear and other squadron equipment which, with thirty squadron ratings, were transferred to *Emperor* by lighter during the night. As they worked, the men

57

of 851 Squadron wondered, with the rest of the Fleet, what had happened to cause all this commotion.

The news was that the Japanese were about to try and put into effect their plans for part of Operation SHO (Akiraka), the evacuation of the Andaman and Nicobar Islands. Initially, the heavy cruiser *Ashigara* and the destroyer *Kamikaze* were due to sail from Singapore, bound for the Andamans, on 10 May. For some time, Allied Intelligence believed that the heavy cruiser involved was *Ashigara*: in the event, she did not take part but stayed in Singapore. On the 19th she was ordered to go to Lingga Roads to carry out exercises with the Army Air Force torpedo aircraft team from 19 to 24 May. The evacuations were actually to be carried out by two groups of ships: Force One (as the Allies named it) consisting of the heavy cruiser *Haguro* and the destroyer *Kamikaze*, and Force Two, the auxiliary supply vessel *Kurishoyo* Maru No 2, escorted by Submarine Chaser No 57. *Haguro*, who had already been reported on 22 April carrying troops from Java to Singapore, and *Kamikaze* were to take food and supplies to the Andamans and to return with the bulk of the garrison there. *Kurishoyo* and her escort were to do the same for the Nicobars.

All these moves were forecast by Allied Intelligence which, by the summer of 1945, had become a finely tuned and sensitive instrument, drawing information from many sources: from the Japanese section of the Operational Intelligence Centre in the Admiralty, based on ULTRA information from penetrated Japanese codes; from Intelligence in Washington; from men of clandestine organizations such as Force 136; from agents in Malaya and Singapore, especially in the Chinese communities, and from Allied staff officers at Naval Headquarters in Colombo and at SEAC headquarters at Kandy, trained to collect and evaluate information from many sources.

For immediate operational purposes, some of the most important and prolific sources of Intelligence were the 'Y' Groups, who were installed ashore at HMS *Anderson* in Colombo and who were also embarked, in parties of three or four men, in many ships down to destroyers. Very early in the war against Japan, at the beginning of 1942, it had been realized in the Admiralty and elsewhere that there was a severe shortage of Japanese linguists in all three services. At that time the Japanese themselves looked upon their own language as a secret racial code, not to be vouchsafed to unworthy outsiders. University graduates were selected to undertake intensive joint-service courses in Japanese. The courses were so intensive that the trainees learned either written or spoken Japanese, it being considered too great a mental burden in the time available to learn both. The embarked 'Y' parties kept radio watches, generally on a special set often known as 'Headache', to monitor Japanese radio frequencies and give rapid and up-to-date information on the movements and intentions of Japanese surface shipping.

In this case, the initial key for the Intelligence information came from ULTRA. In the Far East, as at home, the rules for ULTRA were strictly laid down and enforced. ULTRA intercepts were only sent to Flag Officers and were only handled by a minimum of officers. At Colombo, the number was five; the Deputy C-in-C, Rear-Admiral R. S. G. Nicholson, who was also Flag Officer Ceylon, the Chief of Staff, Commodore M. W. St. L. Searle, and three other officers. ULTRA intercepts could only be transmitted by hand of an officer. (All messages by hand had to be recovered by the delivering officer and destroyed.) By signal, ULTRA information was passed by one-time pad, a system in which a particular cypher was used for one message only and then the cypher table was destroyed. ULTRA signals were not allowed to be transmitted or repeated in any other form, or referred to, however obliquely. If any action was taken on ULTRA information which was likely to compromise the source, i.e. a too-good-to-be-true appearance of Allied forces at the right place and time to destroy an enemy convoy, then a 'cover story' had to be arranged, such as an aircraft sighting or 'one of our submarines has reported'. Lastly, no officer in the ULTRA secret could voluntarily put himself in any position where he might be captured by the enemy.

In essence, the intelligence summary from ULTRA and other sources on 10 May was that a heavy cruiser of the *Nachi* class was due to arrive at Port Blair in the Andamans before nightfall on 12 May. The enemy's intentions were either to attack Allied forces and shipping off Rangoon, or to reinforce, re-supply or evacuate personnel or material from the Andamans. The enemy cruiser was due to leave Port Blair before daylight on 13 May. Her average mean speed for the passage was estimated to be 25 knots.

On the morning of 10 May the C-in-C, Admiral Sir John Power, flew from Colombo to Trincomalee and went on board the flagship *Queen Elizabeth* to confer with Admiral Walker. Later in the afternoon, the C-in-C embarked in the headquarters ship *Ulster Queen* and sailed for Rangoon, arriving on the 13th. He left Rangoon on the 14th and arrived back in Colombo on the 19th. He was therefore away from his headquarters and at sea for much of the ensuing period. General control of matters at Colombo devolved on Admiral Nicholson, the Deputy, and on the Chief of Staff. However, the C-in-C himself occasionally interposed signals concerning operations 'as from C-in-C in *Ulster Queen*'. This caused the possibilities of a divided counsel and potential confusion.

Admiral Walker had constituted Force 61, consisting of almost every ship available in harbour, which sailed in three groups from 0600 onwards. Group II, of the 21st Aircraft Carrier Squadron, of *Hunter*, *Khedive*, *Emperor* and *Shah*, under Commodore Oliver in *Royalist*, escorted by *Rotherham* (D.11), *Nubian* and *Penn*, sailed first and led the way. Group I, of *Queen Elizabeth* (flag), *Tromp* and *Tartar* followed, while Group III, of *Cumberland*, flying Rear-Admiral Patterson's flag, *Richelieu* and the 26th Destroyer Flotilla (minus *Verulam*) brought up the rear. Shortly after sailing *Penn* had defects in her freshwater distilling plant and returned to harbour. She was replaced by *Tartar*.

Verulam also sailed later: she had been preparing for a boiler clean and was unable to sail with the rest of the flotilla until all the machinery below was 'boxed up' again. All ships in Force 61 had sailed fully replenished, except *Queen Elizabeth*, who was short of some 15-inch ammunition and two of the carriers which were short of aviation fuel. A fuelling group, Force 70, of the tanker RFA *Echodale*, escorted by *Paladin*, also sailed that afternoon.

Force 61 steamed eastwards at 16 knots, on a fine, sunny, calm and 'typically Indian Ocean' day. In the forenoon a signal was passed round the Force that the object of the operation was an anti-shipping sweep to intercept and destroy the Japanese evacuation forces for the Andamans and the Nicobars. The intention was to catch up with the enemy some time on Saturday, 12 May. The operation was later codenamed DUKEDOM.

The heavy cruiser *Haguro* (Captain Kaju Sugiura) left Singapore on 9 May, escorted by *Kamikaze* (Lt-Commander Kinichi Kasuga) and two submarine chasers, with an air escort of three 'Jake' (Aichi 13A) floatplanes from 936th Air Group, based at Sabang, from dawn on the 10th. The first indication Admiral Walker had of the cruiser, and thus the first hard information of the nature of the quarry, came up at 10.30 pm that evening when a signal was received from *Subtle* (Lieutenant B. J. B. Andrew), one of three submarines on patrol in the Malacca Strait, reporting a *Nachi* Class heavy cruiser, painted pink and green, escorted by one destroyer and two other escorts, steering 315 degrees, at 17 knots. Sightings of 'pink and green cruiser' (actually *Haguro*'s camouflage paint) from submarines so soon after VE Day celebrations might have been regarded with reservations in the flagship, but in fact Andrew had already attempted an attack.

The submarines *Subtle, Statesman* (Lieutenant R. G. P. Bulkeley) and *Scythian* (Lieutenant C. P. Thode RNZNVR) had sailed from Trincomalee on 20 and 21 April to establish patrols in the narrows of the Strait, around the Aroa Islands and One Fathom Bank—an area chosen because lack of sea-room would deny a large enemy ship space to evade, and give submarines a better chance of interception. However, the choice of operating area brought with it disadvantages. Currents of up to six knots ran through the narrow channel at certain stages of the tide. Apart from One Fathom Bank lighthouse itself, there were very few navigation marks. The nearest coastlines were of unbroken green jungle, with few distinguishable features. To help navigation, the submarines carries dan-buoys with flags mounted on top, which they dropped in known positions and used as a datum. But the buoys were difficult to sight through the periscope, and more than once they were 'not watching' i.e. dragged under water by the force of the tidal stream. The submarines had to devise their own solutions. *Subtle* put a McVitie & Price biscuit tin on the buoy, with a captured Japanese flag tied on top. *Statesman* was even bolder and placed an Oldham battery powered light on her buoy. *Scythian*, being nearer the Aroa Islands, had an easier navigation problem and dispensed with her buoy altogether.

There were in fact three channels down the Strait at that point. *Subtle* had the central channel, which ran for some 20 miles N.N.W. along the western edge of One Fathom Bank. It varied in width from 5 to 13 miles. Its maximum depth was about 30 fathoms, with shoaling sandbanks on either side. *Scythian* had the western channel, nearest to the Sumatran coast. It ran for about 55 miles N.N.W. of the Aroa Islands, with a maximum width of ten miles and depth of 30 fathoms. *Statesman* had the most awkward, eastern channel, closest to the Malayan coast. It was bounded by sandbanks and shoals for about twenty miles, with a very narrow navigable channel, and was not much more than 10 fathoms (sixty feet) at its deepest point.

By the 9th Thode in *Scythian* had sighted two minesweepers working his part of the channel and concluded, correctly, that they were preparing the way for something much bigger. He plotted their course carefully, since anything heavier would be bound to follow their route. At 5.30 am that morning all three submarines had shifted patrol area further north in accordance with their patrol orders. When they surfaced to recharge batteries after dark that evening they were ordered to return to their original positions. Their patrol priority was also changed, from 'report then attack' to 'attack then report'.

Andrew, the senior CO of the three, had the best chance in the central channel. For some time on the 10th he and the other COs had observed unusual Japanese air activity, with several aircraft circling above the horizon to the southward. It was a sure sign that something was coming their way. At 4.40 pm Andrew put up a periscope and, with a dry mouth and a thumping heart, sighted the fighting tops and funnels of a heavy warship. She was steaming north, towards *Subtle*, along the centre channel. In a few more minutes Andrew could see that she was escorted by two submarine chasers, ahead of her, and on either bow. By 5 pm *Subtle* was approaching to an attacking position, so close that Andrew could see Japanese sailors on the cruiser's upper deck. As his target stood on towards him Andrew was struck by her beauty. She was, in his words, 'a very sleek beautiful ship' and moreover she was slowly moving into a perfect target position. At four minutes past five, when the range was 1,200 yards and coming down rapidly, Andrew opened his mouth to give the order to fire when the target turned sharply to starboard through 60 degrees and headed north-east, leaving Andrew with a very difficult stern shot. Some sixth sense, some inkling of his danger, must have warned the Japanese captain, who turned just in time. As his target, which was *Haguro*, went past, Andrew noticed a destroyer astern of her. Bitterly disappointed and frustrated, Andrew broke off his attack, and ordered *Subtle* to a depth of ninety feet. To his surprise and alarm, *Subtle* hit the bottom at thirty-five feet. Had torpedoes been fired, they would almost certainly have hit the nearest sandbank.

Haguro's turn away took her towards *Statesman*. Bulkeley had sighted smoke to the south-west at 5.11 pm and had also prepared for an attack. But *Haguro* simply would not come close enough. Bulkeley brought *Statesman* shallower and shallower to get a better view and at one point his periscope was sticking more than ten feet out of the water. He could see *Haguro*'s upper-works and mainmast as he turned north-east to try and pursue. But a submerged submarine had no chance at all with a ship doing an estimated 17 knots. *Haguro*'s underwater propeller noises began rapidly to fade from *Statesman*'s sonar listening receiver and by 6 pm Bulkeley had lost all contact. *Statesman* then surfaced to transmit her enemy sighting report. The message was not received because of defective radio equipment but happily *Subtle* had also surfaced to send a report and her message was safely received in *Queen Elizabeth*.

As *Haguro* and her escorts moved off to the north, the submarines were left behind and out of the action for the time being. The prolonged running at high speed during the day had overheated *Statesman*'s battery and every time a charge was tried the battery temperature soared above the safety limit, and the charge had to be broken off. The battery was still not completely charged by daybreak, but Bulkeley took a chance and stayed on the surface to finish charging. Luckily, *Statesman* was not sighted.

Meanwhile, in *Scythian* over to the west, Thode had not sighted *Haguro* nor intercepted any messages about her, but he had had his own excitements. On the 11th he sighted two Japanese Landing Craft (Infantry), steaming north through his channel. *Scythian* surfaced and the targets were engaged with main and secondary armament. The Japanese quickly returned a very accurate fire. They scored two 6-pounder hits on the submarine's casing. A third shell damaged the plating of the conning tower. One shot in the pressure hull from this sort of opposition might prevent *Scythian* diving, so Thode broke off gun action and dived. *Scythian* ran out at high speed to a point on the LCIs' beam, where she could outrange them. The submarine surfaced again and this time both LCIs were sunk in a few salvoes.

Once he had *Subtle*'s enemy report, Hookey Walker could make some plans. Depending upon later enemy reports, he decided to head for the Ten Degree Channel and be astride it by the night of

11/12 May, ready to intercept the cruiser on her way north. Failing that, he could have his force in the Six Degree Channel and intercept the following night.

At dawn on the 11th the whole of Force 61 was heading eastwards towards the Ten Degree Channel. But there were delays. *Shah* reported fuel contamination and had to slow down to 6 knots, *Nubian* being detailed to escort her. In very light winds, the force had to manoeuvre to launch and land on aircraft for the Combat Air Patrol (CAP) and by noon on the 11th it was obvious that Force 61 could not reach the Ten Degree Channel in time. At half past twelve, the whole force altered course to the southeast, to head for the Six Degree Channel.

Almost at once there was a 'bogey' on *Queen Elizabeth*'s radar screens, range 84 miles, bearing north. Two Seafires were detached from *Hunter*'s CAP and vectored out on the bearing, but they saw nothing.

Two ULTRA intercepts on 11 May revealed that the Japanese had flown special air reconnaissance flights that day, two in the morning from Port Blair to a depth of 200 miles to the north-west and west of the Andamans, and a third in the afternoon from Car Nicobar to a depth of 200 miles north-west of the Nicobars. It was almost certainly one of the Port Blair flights which *Queen Elizabeth*'s radar screens had detected, but it was probably the Car Nicobar flight which actually sighted part of Force 61 later in the day. This was revealed by another ULTRA intercept on the 12th: 'One heavy enemy ship sighted by air recco'. Shortly afterwards, a fourth ULTRA intercept showed that the *Nachi* Class cruiser had been ordered to return to Singapore.

A Japanese Army reconnaissance aircraft certainly had sighted part of Force 61 and reported that the Allied force consisted of one escort carrier, one cruiser and several other ships. That was enough. Captain Sugiura turned back, just as he had been ordered and as Admiral Walker had been afraid he would, and headed south for the Malacca Strait again. A suicide *kamikaze* attack by ten Japanese Army aircraft was planned for the next day, 12 May, and *Haguro*'s future movements would depend upon the success or otherwise of this attack.

At 2.30 pm on the 11th all but one of 851 Squadron's Avengers began to fly off from *Shah* and transfer to *Emperor*. Each aircraft was de-bombed and defuelled down to 80 gallons, to make it light enough to take off without the accelerator. *Emperor* received her guests in good spirit, but she was a 'fighter' carrier, not worked up for torpedo-bomber operations, and her operations room crew were strangers to 851. This, too, had a bearing on the action to come.

Hellcats were transferred from *Emperor* to *Shah* to balance the numbers of the respective flight decks. 851 Avengers were briefed at 9 pm that evening for a possible anti-shipping strike, but stood down. The crews were to stand by, all day, for the next two days, without being required.

Realizing that he had almost certainly been sighted, Admiral Walker still hoped that if he held his ships away unobtrusively to the southward, the enemy might gather courage for another sortie. Meanwhile, he did detach Group III, of *Cumberland*, *Richelieu* and the 26th Destroyer Flotilla (which now included *Verulam*) after dusk on the 11th, when there was no risk of air detection, to steam at 21½ knots so as to be in the Six Degree Channel by dawn on the 12th. Admiral Walker believed (wrongly) that there was still a faint hope of catching *Haguro* on her way.

Haguro and *Kamikaze* had indeed turned back into the Malacca Strait where once again they were sighted by the submarine patrol line and, once again, Andrew was 'in the pound seats', with another good chance of a shot. *Haguro* was sighted at 6.40 am on the 12th. She still had her destroyer escort, and her air cover of three Jakes was back again. But this time *Haguro* was making at least 25 knots and zigzagging violently, altering up to 20 degrees either side of her main estimated course of about south-east.

By great good fortune, *Subtle* was actually not too far off *Haguro*'s mean line of advance but the vigorous alterations in course made it difficult for Andrew to set up his attack. Finally, at 7.06 am he fired a full bow salvo of six torpedoes at a range of 2,500 yards—not as close as he would have liked but it should have been close enough—and then went deep, or at least as deep as the Malacca Strait allowed, being about ninety feet.

The sea was glassy calm, and the torpedo tracks were sighted, probably from *Haguro* herself, although the aircraft may also have warned her. *Haguro* turned right away to port leaving *Kamikaze*, who had been given an excellent datum position by the torpedo tracks, to deal with *Subtle*.

Subtle, on her way down, struck bottom at about 65 feet and lay there, apparently an easy target for the attacking destroyer. To his intense disappointment at having been given two bites at such a large and juicy cherry—a target out of a submariner's favourite dreams—Andrew now had added the real anxiety of a steady determined and methodical depth-charge attack which lasted intermittently for almost three hours. Andrew attempted to shift *Subtle*'s position, working the screws whenever a fresh depth-charge salvo muffled the noise, but the destroyer seemed to have *Subtle*'s measure and ran in again and again for another attack.

Over to the east, Bulkeley was doing his best to help. *Statesman* had first detected *Haguro*'s propeller noises at 6.20 that morning and Bulkeley had sighted the tips of *Haguro*'s masts through his periscope at 6.42, two minutes after Andrew. Bulkeley, too, had been in the initial stages of an attacking approach when *Haguro*'s violent turn away to avoid *Subtle*'s torpedoes threw his calculations and predictions completely out. *Haguro* eventually steamed safely past *Statesman* at a range of over 9,000 yards and all Bulkeley could do was to notice that she had her two submarine chaser escorts back astern of her again. He now turned his attention to *Kamikaze*, but every attempt to set up an attack on her was foiled by her rapid changes of course as she went about her business of bombing *Subtle*. It was like trying to hit a fast-moving boxer with a dart thrown from outside the ring. *Kamikaze* did not drop any charges nearer *Statesman* than 3,000 yards although she actually passed right over *Statesman* more than once. Clearly the enemy did not suspect there were two submarines present.

Eventually *Kamikaze* moved away, evidently satisfied that *Subtle* had been dispatched. But *Subtle*, although Andrew and his ship's company had endured a very uncomfortable time, and the submarine herself had suffered considerable internal damage to machinery, fittings and gauge glasses, did survive, and managed to surface after dark that evening.

Once on the surface, Andrew had great difficulty in opening the top conning tower hatch. He had to use all his strength and get the signalman to assist him before he could lift it, because of the weight of the great heaps of sand and silt dredged up by the depth-charge explosions and deposited on the submarine's bridge and conning tower hatch. Steaming and navigation lights, and the bridge gyro compass repeater were all smashed. *Subtle* tried to send off an enemy sighting report but her radio gear and aerials had also been damaged by the explosion, and the message was never transmitted.

In the meantime Force 61 steamed east at 17 knots. Admiral Walker had had no reports from submarines, although they had been in action, nor from Liberators flying patrols in the Andaman Sea. By 11.20 am, on 12 May, Admiral Walker had definitely concluded that their quarry had been alarmed and would not venture out until everything was quiet again.

Commodore Searle, the Chief of Staff in Colombo, had also deduced from ULTRA intercepts that the *Nachi* cruiser was returning to Singapore and could arrive there on 14 May. At noon he signalled to Walker: 'You have been sighted. Your target returning to base. Assume you will return to area of Position "Q" [about 200 miles south-west of Achin Head] and await news.' Admiral Walker ordered Group III to rejoin and led Force 61 to the Position 'Q' area, to rendezvous with Force 70.

Allied Intelligence had got wind of Japanese intentions of a suicide attack and warned Admiral Walker who was already greatly concerned about the safety of the fuelling Force 70, then passing closer to the Nicobars. As it was quite possible that the Japanese 'snooper' had sighted Force 70 as well as part of Force 61, Force 70 was ordered to steam south-west at full speed and to be ready for suicide attacks (which, happily, never developed, either against Force 70 or Force 61). A fuelling rendezvous was fixed for 13 May.

To keep the enemy preoccupied, Admiral Walker decided to launch strikes against the airfields at Car Nicobar. That morning's flying, in its incidents and accidents, was very typical of East Indies Fleet air operations at the time. *Emperor* launched four Hellcats fitted with long-range fuel tanks, at 11.33. To avoid radar detection they flew at 500 feet to a point some 50 miles from the islands. Some 15 minutes after passing this point, the pilot of one of the Hellcats, Sub-Lieutenant W. Willis RNVR, reported that his engine was overheating and his aircraft had developed electrical faults. Soon afterwards, Willis' radio also failed and his section leader, Sub-Lieutenant N. Painter RNVR, decided to accompany Willis back to *Emperor*.

The two remaining Hellcats went on and carried out a brisk and successful attack. In the face of some inaccurate flak from the rim of the south-west airfield on Car Nicobar, they swept across the runway and shot up a petrol bowser and a lorry, setting both on fire. At a second airfield they strafed a small convoy of lorries moving round the strip perimeter and then concentrated their fire on a Nakajima B6N2 (Jill) torpedo-bomber, brand new in its gleaming fresh paint, standing at the end of the runway. That, too, was set on fire. As the Hellcats were withdrawing they were unexpectedly fired on from two light AA positions beside the hangar. They dived down again and silenced both guns with their cannon fire, killing or wounding the crews. It was, ironically, precisely the type of strafing attack, unmolested from the air, which the Japanese Zeros themselves had carried out so effectively in the skies above Malaya and Singapore in 1942.

Meanwhile, Force 61's radar sets had picked up a 'bogey' and *Emperor* flew off four Hellcats at 12.25 to investigate. However, their interception broke down and all four were diverted to land on *Shah*, while another section of four Hellcats was ranged on deck. These began to fly off at 2.30 pm but as they took off one Hellcat crashed over the side into the sea. The pilot was picked up by *Royalist*. A fifth Hellcat was launched as the surviving three were returning to land on *Shah*. The last of this trio caught its arrester hook on the rear fairing of the after lift instead of in an arrester wire. The hook was torn out and the Hellcat, with its landing speed still almost undiminished, smashed through both safety barriers and into the deck-park of Hellcats on the forward flight deck. All but one of the aircraft was damaged beyond *Shah*'s capacity to repair them but very fortunately nobody was hurt. The day's adventures proved once again that operational accidents cost the Fleet Air Arm far more aircraft than the enemy.

The excitements of the 'bogey' and the manœuvrings to launch and land on aircraft had taken Force 61 almost 100 miles to the south of where the returning Hellcats from Car Nicobar had expected to find it. The Hellcats climbed to 12,000 feet and picked up the carrier's homing beacon at a range of 85 miles (well over the maximum range for that set at that height) and landed on safely at 4.05 pm.

The weather, too, was an unpredictable adversary. In monsoon weather violent rain squalls sprang up apparently from nothing, giving neither ships nor aircraft much warning. One CAP of four Hellcats from *Khedive* that day, led by Lieutenant S. J. K. Edwards, RNVR, were orbiting round the carrier at 700 feet, preparing to land on, when a particularly vicious squall blew up. Edwards and his flight switched to instrument flying and clustered into a tight formation for mutual encouragement and guidance, according to standard practice. But the minutes passed, their remaining fuel supply dwindled and still the squall held them. After one pass overhead, and another circuit, while anxiety rose in

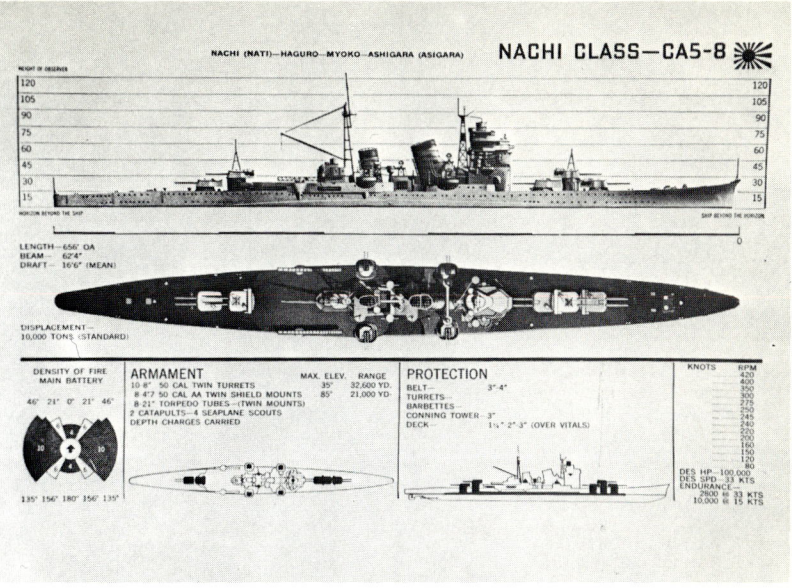

1 Details of Japanese *Nachi* Class heavy cruisers, as published in Allied Intelligence publications, 1945.

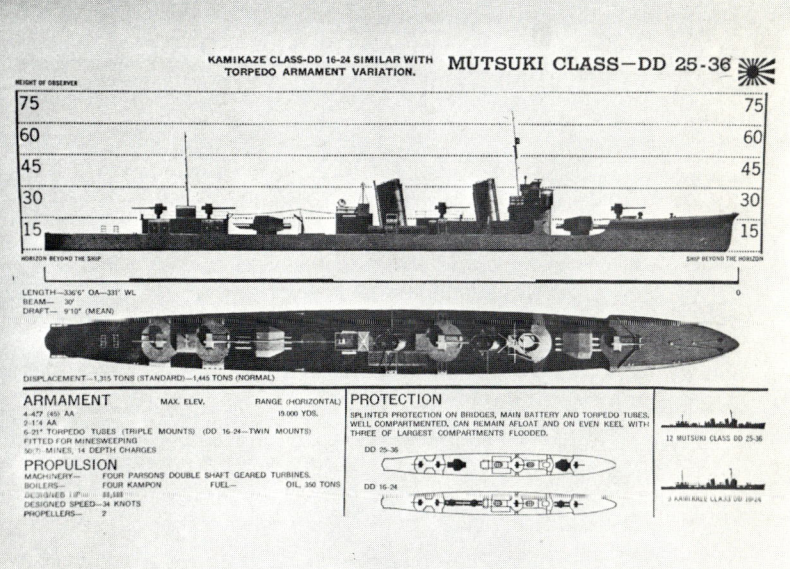

2 Details of Japanese *Mutsuki* and *Kamikaze* Class destroyers, as published in Allied Intelligence publications, 1945.

3 The heavy cruiser *Haguro*.

4 The destroyer *Venus*.

5 Stewart Sound, 19 March, 1945. The *Rapid*, hit in both boiler rooms. A smoke float has been dropped on her starboard side in an attempt to hide the ship from a Japanese shore battery.

Khedive, the Hellcats were still invisible in the clouds. At last, after what seemed an interminable period, Edwards and his section managed to land on safely, all of them admitting they had been 'shaken rigid'.

After breaking off her action with *Haguro* for the second time, *Statesman* again had troubles with overheating battery cells and Bulkeley surfaced as soon as it was safe. He succeeded in transmitting a sighting report: 'Cruiser and three destroyers [*sic*] steering 180 degrees 18 knots at 0845 this morning'.

Admiral Walker received this signal at about 3 pm that afternoon, half an hour after he had the latest intelligence summary from Colombo. This appreciation of the situation suggested that, had *Haguro* pressed on, she would have reached the latitude of 11°, just south of the Andamans, by noon on the 12th. But as no air reconnaissance or Intelligence intercepts had given any further information about her, it was very probable that she had doubled back into the Malacca Strait. This, and *Statesman*'s signal, both pointed the same way. Admiral Walker took his force south to fuel and await developments. Meanwhile the Chief of Staff had assumed that the operations might be protracted. The cruiser *Nigeria* had just reached Trincomalee from Simonstown. She was ordered to put to sea as soon as she had refuelled, with *Roebuck*, *Racehorse* and *Redoubt*, forming Force 62, which sailed early on the 13th. They were joined on the 14th by *Rocket*, who had left Trincomalee on 9 May escorting Convoy WO5, of two troopships, bound for Geraldton in Western Australia. The troopships were left to go on alone. *Penn* had rectified her defects and sailed on the 13th with the tanker *Olwen*, forming another fuelling group, Force 67. The operational plot at Naval HQ in Colombo now showed a picture of overwhelming force, hurrying eastwards, to wait for *Haguro* north of the Malacca Strait.

At this point the picture was nearly spoiled by the Commander-in-Chief himself, Admiral Sir John Power, by this time in Rangoon in *Ulster Queen*. During the afternoon of the 12th he signalled the cruiser *Phoebe*, who had been patrolling the coast of Burma off Mergui with six frigates of the Royal Indian Navy, to end her patrol and close Port Blair, unless otherwise ordered by Admiral Walker. Admiral Walker replied that he feared *Phoebe* would alarm the enemy and he would much prefer her to return to Trincomalee. Commodore Searle, the Chief of Staff, then confirmed Admiral Walker's signal, as though it had come from and with the authority of the C-in-C. But the episode had been a perfect example of how remote control could ruin the plans of men on the spot. Luckily, this time, no harm was done.

Group III rejoined Force 61 that evening of 12 May, after having had some difficulty in finding the main force. *Eskimo* was detached to meet Force 70 and escort it to the fuelling rendezvous. Fuelling began early on 13 May in monsoon weather, with squalls and pouring rain, which were so bad that flying had to be cancelled.

Most of the Force 61 destroyers fuelled from the carriers that day. *Virago* had another brush with a carrier, this time *Emperor*. *Saumarez*' navigating officer, Lieutenant Hugh Knollys, afterwards drew a cartoon showing an emperor in knee breeches and buckled shoes, dancing on one irate toe, crown flat aback and coat-tails flying, being savaged in the backside by a three-stripe Wren officer; the caption was Power's signal to *Virago* at the time: 'You really must be more careful how you approach these great men!' *Emperor* also indulged in some frivolous signalling with *Venus* while refuelling and replenishing her with fresh bread. *Emperor* to *Venus*: 'When purple emperors toil by day and night providing bread and oil for Venus, how should the lady pay?' To which *Venus* replied: 'The lady always pays, but virtue has its own reward'. Captain Power, in *Saumarez*, hearing this exchange by TBS (TBS: Talk Between Ships short-range radio) from some distance away, interjected: 'Can't take you in her arms because she hasn't got any'.

After this somewhat Delphic exchange, which would certainly have baffled any Japanese equivalent of a 'Y' Party listening in, the Force carried on fuelling, completing by nightfall. The whole

72

force then steered north-east to pass through the Six Degree Channel at 4 am on 14 May and intercept the enemy, should they make another try. But by 5.15 that morning there had been no sign of the Japanese. Admiral Walker's ships reversed course to return to the fuelling area, but leaving Group III, under Rear Admiral Patterson in *Cumberland*, to wait in the Six Degree Channel.

Actually the Japanese were on the move. Force Two, comprising *Kurishoyo* Maru No 2 and her escort, left Penang on 12 May. Covered by the bad weather and frequent rain squalls of the next two days, the ships reached Nancowry safely, early on 14 May. *Haguro* meanwhile had been waiting with *Kamikaze* off the lighthouse 16½ miles west of Pulo Burnet, marking the southern limit of One Fathom Bank. Encouraged by Force Two's progress, *Haguro* prepared for another sortie, escorted this time only by *Kamikaze* (the submarine chasers almost certainly having had to go back to Singapore to refuel).

Haguro's second sortie was also betrayed by an ULTRA intercept, received during the morning of 14 May, which reported one heavy cruiser being sent from Singapore to the Andamans, although this heavy cruiser was not necessarily the same *Nachi* that the earlier ULTRA intercepts had mentioned. 222 Group RAF was asked to mount long-range searches of the enemy's possible route to Port Blair between the latitudes of 5° and 10° North. At the same time, the Chief of Staff signalled to 'Hookey' Walker: 'Another *Nachi* sortie expected soon. Long-range aircraft searching route'.

But at this point, the careful arrangements which had been made for stationing submarines on patrol to report and attack the enemy broke down. *Statesman* was off station because she had been ordered to take the place of another submarine, *Torbay*, in an operation to retrieve a clandestine party from Dinding Island. *Scythian* had also left her patrol position. As the Japanese had always used *Subtle*'s centre channel, it seemed to confirm that *Scythian*'s channel was mined. So *Scythian* was ordered to join

73

Subtle. But this time *Haguro* and *Kamikaze* used the now un-watched western channel, close to the Sumatran shore, and both passed northwards unseen and unnoticed—except by *Statesman*, who sighted circling seaplanes over the western horizon at 3.36 pm on the 14th, but could not close and investigate.

Kurishoyo Maru No 2, also betrayed by ULTRA, embarked 450 troops from the Nicobars and sailed for Singapore on the evening of the 14th. She was sighted in the Andaman Sea by patrolling Liberators of 222 Group RAF. But neither their reports nor *Statesman*'s reached Admiral Walker. But he did receive the Chief of Staff's signal: 'Air Recce estimates one small escorted transport heading south for Sabang ETA 15th'.

Admiral Walker's force was by that time about 70 miles south-west of Achin Head and some ships were beginning to refuel again. The Admiral had now had no news at all of *Haguro* for over twenty-four hours, but the feeling was gaining strength among his staff that some decisive move could not be far off. Everybody felt that it was all much too quiet to last. Meanwhile, in the early evening of 14 May the 'Y' Parties began to report radio transmissions from minor enemy surface vessel activity around the northern coasts and capes of Sumatra. The possibility that some subsidiary targets might appear during the search for the primary target had been foreseen by the staff and a subsidiary operation, code-named MITRE, an air and surface ship sweep for shipping targets, had been planned. But it was understood that under no circumstances would MITRE be permitted to prejudice the main object of DUKEDOM.

Early on 15 May Allied Intelligence decoded a signal from *Haguro* stating that she was due to do (something) (groups corrupt: possibly arrive) at One Fathom Bank at 1000 Japanese time (Zero minus nine hours) on 16 May. This appeared to con-firm that *Haguro* was about to have another try. It was some hours before Admiral Walker received this Intelligence. In the meantime, with the battleship *Richelieu*, a cruiser and five destroyers in the Six Degree Channel, and the rest of his force, including the carriers, ready in support, Admiral Walker certainly had his ships in the right places. But, with the possibility of the minor operation MITRE, and the signalling that was to involve, the seeds of uncertainty had also been sown.

[4]

0001–2245/15 MAY

THE SIGHTING

STUDYING THE PLOT in the flag bridge of *Queen Elizabeth* in the early hours of 15 May, Admiral Walker and his staff decided there was enough evidence to initiate MITRE, provided everybody concerned knew that it could be called off at any time. At 2.17 am Admiral Walker made the signal Captain Power had been hoping and expecting. To 26th Destroyer Flotilla: 'Attacking Force destroyers raise steam for full speed forthwith'. Half an hour later, the Admiral sent an amplifying signal, addressed to Captain Power, and repeated to Admiral Patterson and Commodore Oliver, ordering him to 'proceed forthwith with his destroyers at 27 knots to search for an enemy auxiliary vessel along a search area some 80 miles long beginning at 6.30 pm that day about 70 miles north-east of Sabang and ending at 9.30 pm, returning by the same route to rendezvous with Force 70. Air search and strike from the carriers would be arranged. The above,' the signal ended, 'may be cancelled'. At 3.11 am Walker emphasized the last point in another signal: 'If cancel MITRE is received from C-in-C East Indies, or B.S.3 [Walker himself], rejoin me'.

In *Saumarez*, the Admiral's signal to proceed had been received by TBS (Talk Between Ships) at 2.40 and reached Captain Power almost at once. It took only a minute or so to plot the positions, a few more minutes to call in the other destroyers of the flotilla from their screening positions round *Richelieu* and *Cumberland* and by 3.10 am they were all on their way. As Captain Power said, 'It had always been my practise to move first and work out what to do later'. It was, in fact, Captain Power's constant pressing on to the east, despite everything, which eventually prevailed over all the hesitations and uncertainties inherent in the operation to come.

At 3.40 the flotilla set course to pass forty miles north of Weh Island, the northernmost island of Sumatra, where the Japanese had a surface radar station. At 5.05 am Rear-Admiral Patterson was sent to support the 26th Destroyer Flotilla with *Richelieu* and *Cumberland*. But at 7.32 Admiral Walker changed his mind and signalled Patterson to return.

So, at dawn on 15 May, the 26th Destroyer Flotilla was quite alone, rattling along ENE at 27 knots, the five destroyers in a circular formation, with ships three cables (600 yards) apart, to provide mutual support against air attack. It was a beautiful morning, with an already hot sun, a slight following wind and the dim blue hills of Sumatra in sight on the starboard bow.

When dawn action stations were over, the ship's companies went to breakfast. At that speed the ships were rattling and shaking in every rivet. It was clear to everybody that something was up. The main broadcast told every messdeck and machinery space that the flotilla was off on its own to search for a convoy of Japanese ships. The thought of the heavy cruiser was still there, in the back of their minds. Writer Alan Parsons, the Captain's Secretary's immediate assistant, whose action duty it was to keep a narrative of events in the Action Information Centre, was less than enthusiastic about the day's prospects, and he was not alone on the messdecks in feeling some misgivings. 'I had not been keen on going out again, least of all against a cruiser when the war was supposed to be over. I must admit that I cherished the hope that we wouldn't find anything—a thought shared by one or two others but certainly not by M. L. Power and his team of staff officers.'

The thought certainly was shared by Leading Steward Marshall, the wardroom wine steward. 'I thought at the time "How lousy if we all got killed after 'our' war was over"—we tended to look on this as the Yankee war.'

77

At 7.50 am four Avenger torpedo-bombers were sighted to the north, flying eastwards low over the sea. These were four of 851 Squadron, launched twenty minutes earlier from *Emperor*. For 851 this was the start of a mixed day of disappointment and achievement, of near-disaster and near-misses, a day which crystallized into the space of a few hours all the frustrations and compensations of flying operational aircraft in the Indian Ocean.

851 had first formed as an Avenger Torpedo-Bomber-Reconnaissance (TBR) Squadron at Squantum, Boston, Massachusetts, on 1 October, 1943. Twelve Avenger TBRs arrived within a week and the Squadron was soon up to its strength of 13 pilots, 13 observers and some 100 ground personnel. The Squadron CO, Lieut-Commander A. M. Tuke, was the only regular RN officer, the others all being RNVR. After preliminary Avenger-type training, the Squadron moved to Norfolk, Virginia, in December, to carry out deck-landing training on board USS *Charger*. In January, 1944, the Squadron moved across the United States from Boston to Alameda, San Francisco, and embarked squadron stores and aircraft in *Shah* on the 14th, sailing the next day. *Shah* crossed the Equator on 22 January, 1944, and reached Willingdon Island, Cochin, via Melbourne and Fremantle, on 23 February.

In April the Squadron became a mixed fighter/TBR outfit when four Wildcats were added, and five fighter pilots joined from 891 Squadron to fly them. The Squadron began its work-up to operational efficiency at Katukurunda, experiencing the usual alarms and excursions and excitements of scores of other Fleet Air Arm Squadrons; their life was one of day and night exercises, inoculations, new faces in the mess, airframe routines and engine changes, leaves in rest camps in Ceylon or East Africa. Their first fatal casualties were in April when an Avenger crashed into the sea while doing a night dummy anti-submarine attack on a fixed flare-illuminated target, and the crew of three was lost. In May another pilot was killed, struck by a Wildcat he was 'batting on' to the runway at China Bay.

On 13 May the squadron re-embarked in *Shah* with twelve

Avengers and four Wildcats and in June operated at sea in company with *Begum*. In July there was another fatal accident, when an Avenger trying to land crashed into *Shah*'s quarterdeck. The pilot and air-gunner were rescued, but the observer was thrown into the sea and lost. An air mechanic later died of burns.

The next month the squadron shared in the killing of its first U-boat. *Shah* and *Begum* were then operating in company as a 'hunter-killer' group in the Indian Ocean. On the afternoon of 10 August, Lieut-Commander Tuke sighted a surfaced U-boat and attacked with depth-charges. Avengers of 851 and 832 in *Begum* continued to patrol over the position and early on the morning of the 12th Tuke sighted the U-boat again and his attack forced the U-boat to surface. The U-boat dived but the group's escorts came up to the spot, which was marked with smoke floats. The frigate *Findhorn* and the Royal Indian Navy sloop *Godavari* soon got a firm asdic contact and sank *U-198* with ahead-throwing 'hedgehog' weapons.

In September Tuke was relieved as CO by Lieut-Commander Michael T. Fuller RNVR, a very experienced TBR aviator. He had been a student at Oxford on an archaeological 'dig' in Corfu when war broke out and after an adventurous trip home through wartime Europe he joined the Navy as an ordinary seaman in May, 1940. His flying training went back to Miles Magisters and Hawker Hind biplanes. He had flown Swordfish with Eugene Esmonde (who won a posthumous VC attacking *Scharnhorst* and *Gneisenau* in the Channel in February, 1942) in 825 Squadron in *Victorious*. He had been on board *Victorious* for the *Bismarck* episode but, being the 'junior boy' of the Squadron, did not get a flight. He then transferred to 820 Squadron and flew from *Formidable* in the Indian Ocean at the time of Nagumo's raid in April, 1942 and later as anti-submarine cover for the TORCH landings in North Africa in November. He had been Senior Pilot of the Torpedo Training School at Machrihanish, on the Mull of Kintyre, before doing Avenger-type conversion training in June, 1944, and finally joining *Shah* at Aden.

After some time operating off the coast of East Africa, *Shah* returned to Colombo in October. In theory, 851 was a torpedo squadron, but none of the East Indies Fleet's carriers had any torpedoes and the Squadron practised with bombs and depth-charges. All their experience in the Indian Ocean had been in convoy defence, searching for U-boats. To Fuller and his men, the very word 'convoy' suggested an *Atlantic* convoy—an armada of some eighty or ninety ships, with escorts, stretching almost from horizon to horizon. 'Convoy' in the Japanese meaning of the word in 1945, a gaggle and taggle of two or three miscellaneous small ships, assembled haphazardly as they were available, was a strange concept to 851.

Having stood by for action all day on the 12th and 13th, 851 were finally warned at 9 pm on the 14th to be ready to carry out a search for a Japanese convoy at daybreak on the 15th. The Avenger crews were called at 3 am for briefing. *Emperor*, being an assault CVE, with primarily fighter operating experience, was therefore not used to operating Avenger TBRs, and there was inevitably a certain lack of understanding and *rapport* between aircrew and ship's staff who were strangers to each other. However, *Emperor*'s crew did their best by their guests and their Operations Officer Lieut-Commander Reed, himself a TBR pilot, and his staff worked throughout the night to prepare the preliminary chart-work for 851 Squadron's observers.

The four Avengers were briefed to fly in close formation for 120 miles to a datum point, marked as 'BB' on their knee-charts, which was about midway between Weh Island and Great Nicobar. They were then to fly at 1000 feet for a further 140 miles on individual tracks, each diverging 8° from the next, fanning out to search between the bearing of 044° (almost due north-east) and 068°. When an aircraft sighted the enemy convoy, it was to report its position, and then wait until the other three closed up. All four Avengers would then mount a co-ordinated dive-bombing attack. This 260-mile search range was criticized by the aircrews. It was near their extreme operational range. If the enemy were sighted towards the end of the 140-mile search legs, or near either of the outer limits of the fan, aircraft would have little fuel left to group and attack. However, all four Avengers, each armed with four 500 lb bombs, and designated Duty 'Able', 'Baker', 'Charlie' and 'Dog', were launched by accelerator and were airborne by 7.30.

After reaching 'BB' without incident, the four Avengers duly diverged but saw nothing until 9.37 am, when Duty 'Charlie', piloted by Sub-Lieutenant J. G. V. Burns, RNVR, sighted a large landing craft and a submarine chaser bearing 047°, only a few miles distant. This was *Kurishoyo* Maru No 2 and her escort, heading for Singapore. Duty 'Able', piloted by Lieutenant K. Crompton, RNVR, had picked up VHF transmissions, very much scrambled due to interference, at 9.33 and then at 9.37 heard Burns' sighting report. At 9.45 Crompton altered course to intercept.

Burns shadowed the enemy until 9.50 and then, as no other aircraft had appeared or seemed to have received his sighting report, and fuel was running low, decided to attack alone. He climbed to gain height and speed for his dive and then attacked the larger target, the landing ship. Of his first two bombs, one fell close alongside, but the other 'hung up' and dropped on the second pass.

Burns was now joined by Duty 'Baker', flown by Sub-Lieutenant W. R. P. Bowden, RNVR, who had actually sighted the two Japanese ships five minutes earlier but, thinking of 'convoy' in Atlantic terms, could hardly credit that this was the 'convoy' they were looking for and flew on. Bowden made one attack and dropped all four bombs, without scoring a hit. Burns still had two bombs left and came in again at 1,500 feet to deliver them.

The Japanese gunners were now thoroughly alarmed and alert, and on this last pass Duty 'Charlie' was hit by a cannon shell which exploded in the engine. Oil flooded along the forward fuselage and sprayed over the pilot's canopy so that Burns could see nothing. His Telegraphist-Air Gunner (TAG), Petty Officer A. R. Murley, transmitted a distress signal at 9.55 am: 'Hit in engine—no oil—will continue to fly as long as possible before ditching'. This signal was received in *Shah* and in *Emperor* and both ships tried, without success, to get a direction-finder bearing on the transmission. They also heard Murley's next message 'SOS destroyers ditching' and had no more success in tracing it.

Bowden now formed up on Duty 'Charlie' and transmitted at 9.57, 'One aircraft hit'. Crompton and Rowe-Evans in Duty 'Dog' both heard this signal, followed by Murley's repeated SOS messages. As Charlie's cries of help went on, the listeners heard Duty 'Baker' break into the transmissions with a shout of 'Charlie get your wheels up!'

Duty 'Charlie' was still steadily losing height, in spite of all Burns' efforts. He tried once more to open his canopy, but oil still flooded over his face and helmet and he had to shut it again. Bowden flew down with Burns, as he sank to 500 feet. Murley carried on tapping out his 'SOS . . . SOS . . . SOS . . .' while Duty 'Charlie' dropped lower and lower. When a ditching was inevitable, Burns turned Duty 'Charlie' into the wind and lowered flaps and undercarriage at 50 feet, to increase wind resistance and take as much speed off the aircraft as he could. He raised the wheels again just before Duty 'Charlie' hit the water with an impact that shook every tooth in the crew's heads, bounced quite high, hit again, bounced again, with less height, bounded just clear of the water, came to a stop, and began to settle in the sea.

Duty 'Charlie' was not Burns' crew's normal aircraft and the tiny individual differences in aircraft were enough to cause the crew difficulty in abandoning it. They managed to release the dinghy and inflate it properly but in so doing, the emergency pack, which contained flares, water supply, food and medical equipment, became detached from the dinghy and was lost overboard. However, the three men scrambled safely into the dinghy, just as the tail of Duty 'Charlie' rose in the air behind them, before disappearing for ever. Except for the emergency pack, it had been a model ditching. But the loss of that pack was to have unfortunate results for Burns and his crew.

Bowden circled above them, waving to encourage them, before setting course to return to *Emperor*. He signalled at 10.30 an emergency signal: 'Vessel in distress position [given] mined'. The reference to a mined vessel puzzled *Virago*, who was keeping watch on the aircraft frequency but both Crompton and Rowe-Evans interpreted it correctly. The wrong groups from Naval Aircraft Code had been used.

Having reached his limit of endurance, Bowden set off for home but he too had his adventures. At his estimated time of arrival over the fleet, there were no ships in sight and Duty 'Baker' had 40 gallons of fuel left. Bowden returned to some destroyers he had passed earlier. He could receive no signals on VHF, HF, or either of the homing beacons. He asked the destroyers for a course to steer but could not read the message they flashed to him by light. Bowden dared not gain height, to try to get a reading on the homing beacon, because this might give him away to the shore radar stations. Fortunately two Avengers then appeared and one of them led him towards the carrier. With 30 miles to go, Duty 'Baker' ditched, after being airborne for four hours and 50 minutes. Bowden and his crew got out safely although the swell was much greater than it appeared from above (as Burns had found out when ditching 'Charlie'). Bowden and his crew were picked up by *Hunter*'s Air-sea Rescue Walrus, flown by Lieutenant J. Weaver RNVR. It was a most creditable rescue because the sea conditions were so bad that it was only just possible for the Walrus to land and take off again.

Rowe-Evans had heard Burns' first sighting report. He had expected to hear a further locating report and intended to alter towards the position when he got it. But hearing nothing more, he returned to *Emperor*, landing on at 11.55. Crompton had heard Duty 'Baker's' wrongly coded signal, but read it correctly and closed the given position. He saw nothing, although he must have passed close to Burns' dinghy, and returned to the carrier, landing on at 12.15 (slightly damaging Rowe-Evans' aircraft as he did so). Fuller, the squadron CO, later criticized Bowden for returning to the destroyer instead of heading for the carrier, with only 40 gallons left. However, the aircrews were not wholly at fault. The fleet was some twenty miles west of its expected position. The aircrews had been briefed that the wind was blowing 180° at 10 knots. In fact it was blowing 10 knots at 240° and the aircraft was therefore searching an area to the north-east of where the fleet was expected.

Before ditching, Bowden's TAG, PO T. G. H. Lough, got off another fuller signal at 10.20 which was to have a crucial effect on the whole operation. Referring to the earlier signal of 10.03, Lough gave the position of 'enemy motor vessels, not exceeding 2000 tons'. He added that Duty 'Baker' had attacked two such vessels with dive bombs, but estimated no hits. The signal then repeated the wrongly encoded group about a mined vessel in distress.

This signal, too, was picked up by *Virago* on 6300 k/cs, the aircraft frequency, and passed to Captain Power, but before any action could be taken, or any reference in it queried, or any implications properly appreciated, another signal was received which changed the whole complexion of the operation. It was classified 'Immediate', from the Commander-in-Chief, to Commodore Oliver, Rear-Admiral Patterson, Admiral Walker, and Captain Power: 'Cancel MITRE repeat Cancel MITRE'. According to previous orders, that should have been that. Power's destroyers should rejoin the fleet and the whole operation was off.

The 'Cancel' signal was a result of a meeting, held at Naval HQ Colombo that morning, which had ended within the last hour.

The meeting, attended by Rear-Admiral Nicholson, Commodore Searle, and staff officers, had been arranged (the office buildings of Flag Officer Ceylon were almost next door to Naval Headquarters in Colombo) to consider the operational situation, and particularly Admiral Walker's hunt for the Japanese heavy cruiser, in the light of the latest information. The meeting was told that, from a study of the intercepts, Admiral Walker was clearly just about to detach a force to look for the cruiser and he could only be forestalled if a signal reached him by 1000 Ceylon time. There was an emergency procedure by which a signal could be sent in time, but the message would have to be short and it would have to be drafted by 9.15.

Commodore Searle advised Rear-Admiral Nicholson against any attempt to intercept the cruiser. He said that an interception would only be possible if the Japanese were either unprecedentedly stupid or negligent. The cruiser could easily escape by a slight increase in speed, or if this were not feasible, then she could always take refuge in Penang. If she did that, she could well become an embarrassment, because the East Indies Fleet could not maintain surface forces in that area and other counter-measures were undesirable. In any case, Commodore Searle argued, the cruiser's intentions were no threat to the primary object of the East Indies Fleet, which was the support of the campaign in the north. The original aim of Force 61's sortie (later codenamed DUKEDOM) had been to prevent the *Nachi* class cruiser threatening any Allied forces at or on their way to Rangoon. Now that she had retired into the Malacca Strait that object had been achieved. Commodore Searle suggested a signal to Admiral Walker on the lines of 'Assume you will cancel MITRE in the light of (paraphrased) intercept information. Relative positions (of your own and enemy ships) now make interception unlikely. Assume you will now sweep northwards.' (If Commodore Searle's argument were to be taken to its conclusion, then DUKEDOM also should have been cancelled, but, fortunately for Captain Power and his flotilla, that was never done.)

Rear-Admiral Nicholson thought that a penetration of the Malacca Strait would be undesirable and an unjustifiable risk. He agreed with the Chief of Staff but said he would prefer a shorter signal such as 'Advise cancellation of MITRE'. In the event the signal as actually transmitted could not have been shorter: 'Cancel MITRE, (R) Cancel MITRE.' It was drafted at 9.20 am, and rushed to the cypher office for coding. The originator was 'C-in-C East Indies', so it had the force of the Commander-in-Chief's own authority, although Admiral Sir Arthur John Power was still in Rangoon. The meeting then broke up. At noon that day reports from 222 Group RAF aircraft confirmed that the cruiser and her accompanying destroyer were still heading on a southerly course. There was no more information about the disposition of Walker's ships or any more ULTRA intercepts.

Standing on *Saumarez*'s bridge, still speeding eastward some miles off the Sumatran coast, Captain Power studied the C-in-C's 'cancel' signal. He had received it at 1041. He could see by its time of origin that it had been sent off at 0231 ZULU (i.e. Greenwich mean time). Ceylon was seven hours ahead of Greenwich so the signal had been sent at 9.31 Colombo time, 10.31 *Saumarez* zone time. In other words, and this was the most important point, it had been sent before anybody at Naval Headquarters could possibly have known of the targets that Fuller's aircrews had just been reporting only a comparatively short distance off to the north-east (although ULTRA might have forecast their presence).

Captain Power was in a somewhat unusual situation as regards ULTRA. As Captain (D) of the 26th Flotilla he had no access at all to ULTRA intercepts, but in his previous appointments on the staff of Admiral Cunningham in the Mediterranean, he had been a 'full member of the ULTRA club' and his knowledge coloured his interpretation of any orders he received. Thus, he was well aware that ULTRA had been the reason the fleet had set out from Trincomalee in the first place and that ULTRA had to a large extent governed the fleet's movements as *Haguro* had been 'popping to and fro' in and out of the Malacca Strait. When the 26th Destroyer Flotilla had been sent off to look for merchant ships, Power had deduced that it was *known* they would be there. The fact that he had been warned that a cancellation was possible reinforced Power's belief.

So, when the cancellation did reach him after the ships had actually been sighted, Power's problem became acute. What, he wondered, had prompted this cancellation? Was it fear that his

86

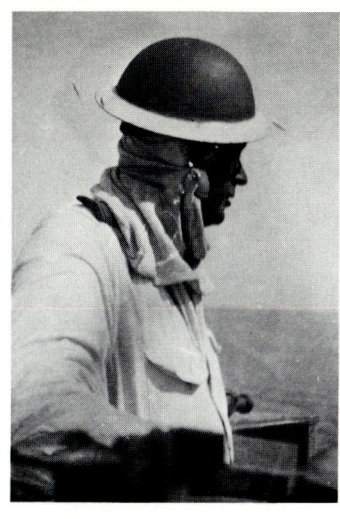

6 Captain Manley Power, Captain(D) 26th Destroyer Flotilla, on the bridge of *Saumarez* during the action in Stewart Sound, 19 March, 1945.

7 Stewart Sound, 19 March, 1945. *Saumarez* with *Rapid* in tow, making smoke to cover their withdrawal.

8 Wreckage and survivors from a Japanese convoy of four ships, destroyed by 26th Destroyer Flotilla in Preparis North Channel, 26 March, 1945.

9 *Verulam*'s 'B' gun bombarding Uleehoe in Sumatra, in company with *Saumarez* and *Vigilant*, 11 April, 1945.

10 851 Squadron, of Grumman Avengers, on board *Shah*, 1945.
Back row (L to R): Rowe-Evans, Fletcher, Burns, Robinson, Handscombe, McEnery, Alexander, Waygood, Ashplant, Odoni, Riordan.
Centre: Bowden, Davy, Eedle, Pemberton, Fuller (Squadron CO), Crompton, Ott, Patterson, Lansdell.
Front Row: Matthews, Griffith, Owen, Whitehead.

destroyers' intrusion would scare the cruiser back into the Malacca Strait and upset Admiral Walker's plans to trap her? Or did Admiral Walker think that the cruiser was too strong for the destroyers on their own? This last was a possibility because the striking force, Group III, had started off with *Richelieu* and *Cumberland*, now some miles in the rear. While reading and re-reading the signal, Power turned the situation over in his mind. What he contemplated doing meant disobeying a direct order. He was desperately worried that by pressing on he might be upsetting the whole plan. Turning a blind eye and going on was all very well for Nelson, but would it spring a carefully laid trap?

Captain Power later wrote of his decision: 'C-in-C's signal, taken in conjunction with other signals addressed to me or intercepted, left me in some doubt, but as it had been originated before the Avengers had reported the enemy I decided to stand on, acting in accordance with Section I, Clause 6 of the Fighting Instructions.'

The sense of this Clause is: 'Very good reasons should exist before touch with an enemy is relinquished. If an order from a senior officer is received, the possibility of the authority not being in full possession of the facts must be considered'. This was another way of expressing Nelson's dictum: 'No officer can do far wrong if he places his ship alongside that of an enemy'. Power decided that, though C-in-C might predict the targets through ULTRA, he could not possibly know they were actually there. So he decided to go on. Captain Power himself called this 'the crucial decision', and so it was. He could have turned back at once and nobody would ever have blamed him. Typically, he chose to go on, and indeed his own staff and all those who knew him would have been astonished if he had turned back. But it still took a man with the courage of his convictions to act as Captain Power did.

Captain Power signalled to the flotilla to reduce speed to 15 knots, since it appeared that they had a few miles in hand. At 10.56 he sent an Emergency signal to Admiral Walker and to C-in-C requesting confirmation of the cancellation, 'in view of aircraft Duty "Baker's" report'. The signal was read at once by *Cumberland*, but there was no response from Colombo although it was transmitted on three separate frequencies three times in the next hour and a half. Eventually, at 12.31, *Cumberland* was asked to pass it on to Colombo. Meanwhile Power flashed the signal to his own destroyers by light: 'Have been recalled. Can afford to ease down a bit pending reply to my application to continue'. Captain Power then amplified his signal of 10.56 with another 'Emergency', again to Admiral Walker and the C-in-C. He repeated Duty 'Baker's' report in more detail, and gave his own position course and speed. His course was 057—*still* north-east, towards the targets Duty 'Baker' had reported.

At 11.50 *Virago* made the electrifying signal: 'Following has been received from Aircraft Duty "George". One cruiser one destroyer bearing 310°.' When Captain Power had the decoded signal in his hand shortly after noon he thumped the bridge rail exultantly with his fists. This one made it all worthwhile. 'In that moment,' he said, 'I had become probably the most relieved man in the Indian Ocean.' Joyfully he ordered the flotilla to increase to 27 knots again and went down to look at the chart. In a few more minutes he had the approval he sought from Admiral Patterson. 'You should sink enemy ships before returning,' Patterson's signal read. 'After landing on air strike Groups 2 and 3 will retire to the westwards.'

Admiral Patterson, too, had the right spirit. In his own report he wrote: 'I felt sure D.26 would continue but in order to clear the matter beyond question and lift the responsibility from him I made a signal instructing him to sink the enemy vessels before returning.' By continuing to stand on to the north-east while waiting confirmation Captain Power had gained a precious forty miles, without which *Haguro* might never have been intercepted.

When he sent his encouragement to Captain Power, Patterson had not yet heard of the cruiser sighting. The enemy vessels he referred to were the two merchant ships Burns and Bowden had attacked. The air strike mentioned was one of four more armed Avengers from *Emperor*, launched at 10.05, and led by Fuller himself.

Fuller's Avenger, Duty 'George', was first off the accelerator of *Emperor* at 10.04. His sortie was to be as beset by chance as Crompton's and Burns' had been before him. While Fuller was circling to wait for the other three Avengers, the report of Duty 'Charlie's' ditching was received in *Royalist*. Commodore Oliver ordered Fuller to stay overhead and wait for further orders. A fifth Avenger was brought up from *Emperor*'s hangar to make up the strike to the original number of four. They were briefed to search on a bearing of 060° for a distance of 200 miles. But it was not to be so simple.

The second aircraft to take off, Duty 'Hotel', had serious engine overheating while waiting to go. She was launched, merely to clear the flight deck, but returned after ten minutes and landed on *Hunter*.

Duties 'Fox', 'Jig', and 'King' were then launched and were at once ordered to jettison their bombs and stay over Force 61. Unfortunately this message was passed on a VHF set which had only recently been installed in the Avengers. The TAGs were not familiar with it and only Duty 'Fox' received the order correctly and complied. Duty 'Fox' circled for an hour and a half, then jettisoned her bombs and landed back on *Emperor*.

Duty 'Jig' and 'King' continued with the search. A possible ditching position had been worked out for Burns' dinghy and this was passed to Fuller who set off at 10.14, followed a minute later by Duty 'Jig' and 'King', to search along a bearing of 070°.

At 10.38, when they were about sixty-five miles along their search route, all three Avengers sighted five destroyers steaming at high speed, course 070°. Fuller closed them under cloud cover, transmitted a brief initial enemy sighting report, but then at 10.45 recognized the destroyers as friendly and cancelled his report. 'Jig' and 'King' were not so perceptive. They too transmitted an enemy sighting report, climbed into an attacking position astern of the destroyers, and tried to identify themselves. The destroyers (who were, of course, the 26th Destroyer Flotilla, now in full cry to the north-east) took no notice. 'Jig' was still doubtful about the destroyers' identities but, after some valuable 35 minutes fuel had been wasted, 'Jig' and 'King' resumed their course. Later, the aircrews protested that the errors were excusable. They had in fact been briefed to expect surface craft. As they had headed for their aircraft before taking off, Lieut-Commander Reed had actually drawn their attention to a blackboard warning them to watch out for the destroyers in a certain position. Reed had only intended a useful caution. But, as he had not thought it necessary to point out that the destroyers would be *British* (believing this to be self-evident) he had evidently left doubt in some minds.

'Jig' and 'King' had barely resumed their base course of 060° when they came upon Bowden in Duty 'Baker', still searching for the fleet after the first strike. Duty 'Jig' broke off the search and escorted Duty 'Baker' homewards until he too ditched, and then landed on *Emperor*.

Duty 'King' pressed on along the search line but the delay and diversions over the destroyers meant that he reached his PLE (Planned Limit of Endurance) some 25 miles earlier than he should have done and so turned for home. When he arrived at his ETA point, there was not a ship in sight. He began a square search, climbing to 5,000 feet. He asked for homing directions on H/F, had a 'Roger' from the operator but then got nothing but the Commodore 21st Aircraft Carrier Squadron's call-sign which continued unceasingly for fifteen minutes. He eventually picked up *Shah*'s YJ beacon at 80 miles and landed on, after 4 hours and 40 minutes in the air, with four bombs and 25 gallons (about 17 minutes flying time) remaining.

Fuller's Duty 'George' was now the only Avenger left. He had not been fooled by the 26th Destroyer Flotilla, although he afterwards noted aggrievedly in his report 'that we had not been briefed that this force was in the area or likely to be encountered'. Fuller flew at 100 feet through the channel between Great Nicobar and Sumatra to avoid radar detection until, just after 11, his observer, Lieutenant A. E. Lansdell RNVR warned him that if they continued to carry the full bomb load, they would only be able to stay in the search area for about twenty minutes. Fuller had previously asked *Royalist* on VHF for some guidance on this point but got no answer. As the primary object of the sortie was now the search for Burns' dinghy, Fuller jettisoned all four bombs. Shortly afterwards, Duty 'George' actually passed within four hundred yards of Burns and his crew in their dinghy, who were unable to signal except by waving frantically and they were not seen.

Emperor's operations room staff had in the meantime worked out a new possible ditching point for Duty 'Charlie' and re-calculated winds and tide and drift to give a fresh search area, more to the westward. They signalled this new area to Fuller but he never received it and flew on to the east. The monsoon weather generally bedevilled radio communications throughout the operation, sometimes giving freakish reception but more often causing black-outs.

At 10.44 Fuller sighted two ships steering 180° at an estimated 10 knots. Coming out of cloud at 1500 feet and closing them, Fuller identified them as a landing ship and a submarine chaser. As he dived from their starboard beam and flew out on their port bow, the submarine chaser opened a light but accurate medium AA and machine gun fire. Now there was no doubt that they were *Kurishoyo* Maru No 2 and her escort. At 10.45 Fuller sent off a brief enemy sighting report and flew down low over the water, ahead of the ships, to shadow them. No sooner had he got out of range of them than he sighted two more ships, 15 miles to the south. He was able to circle them out of gun range and soon identified them as a *Nachi* class cruiser and a *Minekaze* class destroyer steaming north at about 15 knots.

So, almost by accident, *Haguro* had been found. Had Fuller received the amended search area signal he would have flown more to the westward and missed the ships. Admiral Walker had intended to cancel the air searches but he changed his mind and, as he later reported, *Haguro* had been found 'by my own illogical decision to allow the Avenger search to go forward after I had realized that the aircraft would be flown off before the latest time when a signal cancelling MITRE would be received from C-in-C'.

After hours and hours of flying over the sea looking for periscopes, *Haguro* was a 'very big excitement' for Fuller and his crew. 'She was very large and very black against a very dark monsoon cloud. An enormously impressive sight, just as a warship ought to look.' Fuller had set out to find a dinghy and had found a heavy cruiser—who had been anxious not to be found: powerful and beautiful as *Haguro* was, Fuller still had the impression that she had been 'trying to remain unobtrusively out of sight, hoping not to be noticed'. Fuller sent off the sighting report which was received by *Virago* at 11.50 and just after noon began to transmit a stream of vital signals, giving the enemy course and speed, the number of ships and their size in both forces.

As Fuller approached them *Haguro* and *Kamikaze* turned to starboard to a course of 180° parallel with *Kurishoyo* Maru. Fuller climbed to 3,000 feet to transmit his messages, taking up a shadowing position about midway between the two Japanese forces. *Haguro* fired at the Avenger with close-range and anti-aircraft weapons. Fuller could see the flashes rippling and sparkling all along her dark upper decks and around her towering superstructure but he cannily stayed out of range.

At 12.50 Fuller climbed directly over *Haguro* to transmit his last signals giving direction-finders a chance for an exact fix, and took departure a minute later. When Fuller last saw her, *Haguro* was steering 140° at 20 knots. Lansdell gave Fuller a course to fly for home, but Fuller had not been flying long when he felt uneasy and asked Lansdell to check. When Lansdell went over his calculations he discovered he had made a 'rookie' navigator's basic 'rule one' error and given his pilot the reciprocal of the proper course, so that they were flying in exactly the opposite direction to the fleet, towards the Malayan coast. Reversing course, Fuller started on what had now become a very long way home. With a very small margin of fuel remaining and a head wind, Duty 'George' had to be flown as economically as possible, calling for the highest degree of airmanship on Fuller's part.

Neither of the carriers' homing beacons could be picked up but Lansdell managed to fix their position accurately with two running fixes on a point of land at Sabang and they reached the estimated rendezvous position at 2.32 pm to find, as so many aircrews had that day, the sea empty of ships. After flying along the fleet's Mean Line of Advance (MLA) for eleven minutes they asked for a direction-finding bearing. At 2.55 they switched their I.F.F. to 'distress'—the recognized procedure for a lost aircraft 'feeling its way' back to the fleet. A course to steer was passed to them, and two Seafires joined to escort them back. Duty 'George' landed at 3.15 after five hours and 11 minutes airborne, with 15 gallons (about ten minutes flying) to spare, in a position about eighty miles from the estimated rendezvous.

Later, Fuller and his aircrews were critical of the way in which the fleet's MLA, the only method an aircraft's observer had of calculating the fleet's probable position for returning, was several times altered very soon after the aircraft's departure. Fuller pointed out that his squadron might have lost at least three more aircraft by ditching; the three actually landed with less than 20 gallons (about 15 minutes flying) fuel remaining. However, Fuller also blamed himself for over-estimating the operational endurance of his Avengers. He had told the command it was four hours. On reflection, he felt he should have said four hours *unloaded*, three and a half hours loaded.

Fuller himself had flown a model sortie in Duty 'George'. He had been undistracted by changes in plan during flight, or by other aircraft peeling off for other purposes. He had correctly identified the 26th Destroyer Flotilla and had made the correct decision to jettison his bombs. He had found both enemy forces and reported their position, course and speed accurately. He had also brought himself and his crew safely back in the face of further distractions. He was rightly awarded a DSC.

With Fuller's signals, and his debriefing report, in *Emperor*, three more Avengers, designated Duties 'Peter', 'Queen' and 'Roger', were ranged, fuelled and armed for another strike by 1.38 pm. By 1.50 they were on their way—their task, to find and attack *Haguro* and her escorting destroyer.

Two Liberators of 222 Group had also sighted *Haguro* during that afternoon and passed two reports, both of which turned out to be too far to the north. As the second Liberator turned for its base after its final sighting at 2.52 pm it passed over Burns' dinghy at about 500 feet, without seeing it. Once again, Burns and his crew had the bitter experience of waving vainly, and watching the hope of help and safety disappearing rapidly over the horizon. This second Liberator crashed into the sea later, with no survivors.

The Avengers were flown off at a position about 110 miles due west of Sabang. If they had flown direct to their target they would have crossed too close to enemy airfields in Sumatra, so they flew in a 'dog-leg'. Led by Crompton, flying his second sortie of the day, in Duty 'Peter', the Avengers kept a course of 070° at 150 knots for the first 90 miles and then altered to 094° and climbed to 3,000 feet, passing north of the 26th Destroyer Flotilla as they did so. They also sighted *Cumberland* and *Richelieu*, once more steaming to support the destroyers, but still many miles astern of them.

The Avengers were due at the datum position at 3 pm and actually reached it sixteen minutes later. Not surprisingly, *Haguro* was nowhere to be seen, so the aircraft began a 'square search', flying at 140° for 15 miles, turning to 230° for another fifteen, then to 320° for a third fifteen miles. They were nearly at the end of their third leg on a course of 320° when at 3.41 Crompton sighted both *Haguro* and *Kamikaze* on his starboard bow bearing 040°, range about 12 miles, steering a course of due east, speed between 15 and 20 knots. It seemed from the bearing that the enemy must have steamed right into the 'box' of the search area.

All three Avengers had the ships in sight and began to climb to reach an attacking position astern of the enemy, transmitting brief initial and first sighting reports as they climbed. The attackers approached with the sun behind them at 10,000 feet and began their 45° dives at 4.05, 'Peter' and 'Roger' together, 'Queen' some ten to fifteen seconds later. There was no cloud cover below 20,000 feet and therefore no possibility of surprise. *Haguro*'s anti-aircraft batteries soon spotted the aircraft and put up a flak barrage at 10,000 feet which was accurate for height but ahead of the targets. The Avengers weaved and jinked from side to side as they dived through a medium flak attack which scored one hit on 'Peter's' wing and peppered 'Queen's' port wing with splinters. All three bombed from 3,000 feet although Sub-Lieutenant Eedle in 'Roger' found that he had to adjust his tail trim right forward to keep his aircraft's nose down as he dived. *Haguro* was slow in taking avoiding action, appearing to make one leisurely turn to port. The bombers thought they had scored one hit on the fo'c'sle and one near-miss. Actually, *Haguro* was not hit—but may have been diverted to the eastward for a vital few minutes longer. *Kurishoyo Maru* was also almost unscathed by the earlier Avenger attack. She signalled *Haguro* reassuringly that her damage was very small and did not affect her steaming or fighting capacity.

'Peter' and 'Roger' made their getaways, at full throttle, 290 knots, still jinking and weaving at 3,000 feet. 'Queen', flown by Rowe-Evans, carried on down to 300 feet and fled out over the sea on *Haguro*'s starboard bow. Rowe-Evans too was throwing 'Queen' violently from side to side to avoid flak and also the great water columns of bursting eight-inch shells, fired in the hope that the aircraft would fly into the solid wall of water. At one point Eedle felt 'Roger' reacting alarmingly as a shell burst almost beneath them, but he and the other two Avengers got safely away, reforming at 4.15 and setting course for base. On their way back they ran into thick cloud and had to come down close to the sea, but all landed on by 6.30. Eedle did not allow for his Avenger being so very much lighter, with no bombs and much less fuel. He misjudged his landing and crashed into the safety barrier.

The three Avengers had completed a flight of 530 miles, the longest attacking round trip of any carrier-borne Fleet Air Arm aircraft during the war. They had accomplished the first dive-bombing attack by 851 Squadron, indeed the first and only dive-bombing attack by British aircraft on a major enemy warship at sea during the Second World War and the first on a ship of comparable size since two squadrons of Skuas dive-bombed and sank the German cruiser *Konigsberg* alongside in Bergen during the Norwegian campaign in April, 1940—more than five years earlier. Crompton and Rowe-Evans and their crews had spent some $9\frac{1}{2}$ hours airborne. Crompton, Lansdell and Crompton's observer, Sub-Lieutenant F. C. Ott RNVR, were all awarded DSCs. CPO E. J. W. Sherlock and PO A. J. Traverse, Fuller's and Crompton's TAGs respectively, both got the DSM.

With such successes behind them, and *Haguro*'s position now so precisely known, 851 Squadron expected to be called upon for another strike. Their aircraft were ready, the crews eager. But, to Fuller's amazement and anger, no further strikes were ordered. Four Hellcats with long-range tanks were launched at 5.20 to provide CAP for *Richelieu* and *Cumberland*, but there was no more Avenger flying—the reason almost certainly being *Haguro*'s range. Crompton's strike had attacked at 260 miles and reports from Liberators during the afternoon, especially one, who said he was in touch with *Haguro*, putting her range at 280 miles from the fleet, and still opening, suggested that *Haguro* was now beyond aircraft reach. In fact, the Liberator was almost certainly wrong, but Commodore Oliver signalled to *Emperor* and 800 Squadron at 2.27 that afternoon cancelling a proposed fighter-bomber strike. 'I hope, however,' he added, consolingly, 'you may have combat tomorrow if it proves necessary to cover D.26 withdrawing from the Malacca Strait.'

At 12.50 *Richelieu* and *Cumberland* had been ordered once again to steam in support of the 26th Destroyer Flotilla but they were still many miles behind. Twenty minutes later *Tartar* and *Eskimo* had been detached to join *Cumberland* but *Tartar* had to rejoin the fleet because of fuel shortage, and *Eskimo* had even further than the big ships to catch up. The submarines had done their best. The Fleet Air Arm had also done their best. It was now all up to the destroyers.

Power's destroyers had worked back up to 27 knots at 12.10 and were steaming due east. Fuller's position report put the enemy 130 miles from the flotilla on a bearing of 070°. At 1 pm the flotilla altered course to 110° and split into divisions in line abreast, five miles apart, with *Venus* and *Virago* in the 52nd Division to the north, and the 51st Division, *Saumarez*, *Verulam* and *Vigilant*, to the south.

At 1.25 the flotilla passed and exchanged identities with *Statesman*, on surface passage to Ceylon. Bulkeley, standing on his bridge in the hot sunshine, watching the destroyers' huge bow-waves through his binoculars, his look-outs to either side and on the periscope standards above him, reflected upon the situation with mixed feelings. With just a little more luck back in the Malacca Strait, there would have been no need for all this. *Haguro* would by now be safely resting on the mud off Sumatra. Bulkeley was one of the most aggressive and successful submarine commanders in the Indian Ocean. In his fifth patrol in January and February, *Statesman* had sunk or driven ashore two junks, an armed trawler, seven coasters, a small tanker, two lighters and a tug, and quite deservedly had a signal of congratulation from the Admiralty on what Admiral Sir John Power called 'an outstanding patrol'. In her next in March and April, *Statesman* sank an entire convoy of seven armed landing craft. Bulkeley was a man who liked blood for supper but now, as the destroyers' bow-waves reached and washed over *Statesman*'s saddle tanks, he could only signal 'Good Luck' as they went by.

Every man in the flotilla knew they would need all the luck that was going. Lieutenant Denis Calnan summed up his ship's company feelings very well. The prospect of an action had been 'greeted with a cheer and the usual ribald sailor's comment on most things Japanese.

'At first I felt the familiar eager excitement taking hold of me, but as the hours passed the full appreciation of our prospects began to sink in.

'We were all well-blooded and expert in action against aircraft, shore batteries and ships of our own size, but a heavy cruiser was something beyond our experience. We knew that if we met her in daylight our chances would be slim indeed: with her great speed and overwhelming gun power she could destroy the flotilla piece-meal long before we could get close enough to retaliate. My excitement, mounting all the time, became more strongly tinged with apprehension.

'As the heat increased and the day wore on, the men around me —no doubt for the same reasons—fell silent, pale and sweating in their jungle-green action dress.'

The ships in the 26th Destroyer Flotilla were of standard fleet destroyer size of 1800 tons (*Saumarez*, the flotilla leader, was heavier at 1900 tons). All five of the flotilla had been laid down at shipyards with famous names such as Hawthorn-Leslie, Fairfields, and Swan-Hunter at the end of 1942 or the first months of 1943 and completed later in the year: *Saumarez* was first, in July, 1943, and *Verulam* the latest, in December. All five had had experience of escorting convoys to and from Murmansk in the crippling cold and dangers of storm in an Arctic winter. *Saumarez* and *Virago* had taken part in the hunting and destruction of the *Scharnhorst* off the North Cape on Boxing Day, 1943. *Saumarez*, with *Savage*, *Scorpion* and the Norwegian destroyer *Stord* had fired a salvo of torpedoes at the German battle cruiser and received in return a shell from *Scharnhorst* which hit her director tower, killing three men and putting the tower out of action. A near miss shook up her engine-room and damaged her forced lubrication system.

Venus, the eleventh ship of her name in the Royal Navy, had joined the 26th Destroyer Flotilla under Captain Power's predecessor in November, 1943, and while escorting Convoy JW56B on 30 January, 1944, had picked up *Hardy*'s survivors, including Captain (D) Geoffrey Robson himself, and later the same day sank *U.314* in company with *Meteor* and *Whitehall*. In April and May *Venus* escorted the fleet carrier *Victorious* on two operations of air strikes against shipping and harbours along the Norwegian coast. In April *Virago*, *Vigilant* and *Verulam* escorted the Home Fleet forces for Operation TUNGSTEN, the Fleet Air Arm attacks on *Tirpitz*.

All five destroyers were present at the D-Day landings in Normandy on 6 June, 1944. *Saumarez* was Senior Officer, 23rd Destroyer Flotilla, giving gun support to Force 'S' in the assault at Ouistreham. *Venus* escorted Convoy J9 to the beaches and then lay off and bombarded defences west of Courseulles. *Virago*, in Force 'S', escorted the Headquarters Ship HMS *Largs* to the 'Sword' area and bombarded the beaches at Lion-sur-Mer. *Verulam* was one of the bombarding ships of Force 'D' and *Vigilant* (the 19th of her name in the Royal Navy) in Force 'J', bombarding targets at Langrune-sur-Mer in support of the assaulting troops of the 8th Canadian Infantry Brigade.

Later in the year *Saumarez* with another destroyer, *Onslaught*, engaged a convoy of three or four German minesweepers and a merchant vessel off St Peter Port, Guernsey on 14 August. The enemy ships were damaged but also inflicted slight damage and some casualties on the destroyers. In October *Venus* escorted the aircraft carrier *Implacable* and the cruiser *Mauritius* on an anti-shipping sweep off the Norwegian coast between Trondheim and Narvik. *Implacable*'s aircraft sank four ships, drove ashore another two and a U-boat, damaged and set on fire another nine ships. Between 11 and 13 November, *Verulam* was one of four destroyers escorting the cruisers *Kent* and *Bellona* on an anti-shipping sweep of the Norwegian coast. Acting on Intelligence from an ULTRA intercept, the force encountered a German convoy of four ships and six escorts off Lyster Light, south-east of Egersund. They sank two of the ships and all but one of the escorts. *Verulam* herself was hit during the action, with two dead and five wounded.

After repairs and refits, and further Arctic convoy escort duties, *Saumarez*, *Venus*, *Virago* and *Vigilant* all left the United Kingdom for the Far East at various dates in January, 1945, arriving at Trincomalee in February. *Verulam* was delayed, repairing her Lyster Light action damage, and did not leave UK until March arriving at Colombo on 1 April. All the ships in the flotilla had a large 'V' in black paint on both sides of their funnel. Some 'V's were vertical, some sloped with the funnel, one was edged in white. The size of the 'V' was laid down as 4 foot by 3 foot, but *Verulam* misread the signal and arrived on the Station with a 'V' 14 feet high. Eventually the flotilla standardized their 'V's as sloping with the funnel and outlined in white—and very 'tiddly' they looked.

The 26th was always a most happy flotilla. The officers and men who served in it all remember their ships and their service with great satisfaction. In *Verulam*, for instance, her first ship's company quickly noticed that the figures of her building Job Number at Fairfields, 11074, added up to thirteen. But those who served in her are unanimous that she was always a lucky and a happy ship.

It was also a most experienced and battle-hardened flotilla. As Calnan rightly said, they were all well-blooded in action and, with their service in European waters followed by their actions in the Indian Ocean, they had been almost constantly at work. Many of the ships' companies, and especially the majority of the senior ratings, the backbone of the ship, had served in their ships since first commissioning.

The officers, too, had plenty of destroyer experience. Douglas Bromley was the junior commanding officer in the flotilla but he had been at sea for almost the whole war and *Verulam* was his fourth wartime sea command. Graham de Chair, the son of Admiral Sir Dudley de Chair, had in *Venus* his eighth seagoing destroyer command in ten years. He had already won a DSC, in command of the destroyer *Vimy*, when she, *Pathfinder* and *Quentin* together sank *U-162* in the Caribbean on 3 September, 1942. *Venus'* First Lieutenant, Peter Meryon, also had a DSC, won as a Sub-Lieutenant in the destroyer *Wrestler* for boarding and obtaining secret information from the captured Italian U-boat *Durbo* in the Mediterranean in October, 1940. For good measure, *Saumarez'* First Lieutenant, Tony Tyers, also had a DSC, won for gallantry in the face of the enemy, as the citation had it, for 'general good works' as the recipient calls it, in the sloop *Enchantress* in the Mediterranean and in the Atlantic. Another member of *Saumarez'* experienced bridge team, Lieutenant Hugh Knollys, the Navigating Officer, had won his DSC in the minesweeper *Harrier* off the Normandy beaches in June, 1944. Bill Argles, *Vigilant's* captain since commissioning, wrote of the flotilla's spirit that 'to plagiarize a saying of another rather more famous naval person—"we were a band of brothers".'

The man responsible for that spirit, the man who set the tone of the flotilla, and who led it into action, was the Captain D.26, Captain Manley Power CBE, DSO. Manley Laurence Power, the son of Admiral Sir Laurence Power, was born in January, 1904, and joined the Navy as a Cadet in September, 1917. Between the wars he joined the Submarine Service, where he was very well thought of; Commodore Searle remembered him 'as the best Number One [in *L.53*] in the 2nd Submarine Flotilla when I first met him'. In due course Power commanded his own submarine, *H.32*, from 1933–35 and then the large *River* Class submarine *Severn* from 1937–39. In 1939 Power was promoted and appointed as a very junior commander to the staff of the C-in-C Mediterranean, Admiral Sir Andrew Cunningham.

As Staff Officer (Operations), Power was A.B.C.'s right hand man in the early days of the war in the Mediterranean, in the operations off the Western Desert, the campaigns in Greece and Crete, and the defence of supply convoys for Malta. He played a large part in the planning for the Fleet Air Arm strike on the Italian battlefleet at Taranto in November, 1940. At that time the

Mediterranean was the centre of strategic gravity in the naval war, and Power was at A.B.C.'s shoulder, to plan, to advise, to comment, to organize, in those early days when the Navy had no allies in the Mediterranean theatre. He was with Cunningham on *Warspite*'s bridge in March, 1941, when the battlefleet surprised and overwhelmed the Italian cruisers *Pola, Zara* and *Fiume* in the night action off Cape Matapan. It was Power who had bet his Admiral ten shillings that they *would* sight the enemy that trip and it was Power, one of nature's winners, who duly pocketed the ten-shilling note. It was also Power, in Cunningham's words, 'an ex-submariner officer and an abnormal expert at recognizing the silhouettes of enemy warships at a glance' who looked through his binoculars and 'pronounced the enemy ships' to be 'two *Zara* Class 8-inch gun cruisers with a smaller cruiser ahead', an exactly correct identification.

Power was well aware that staff officers were often accused of being good planners, but poor doers, able to criticize where they could not themselves perform. He himself took the greatest professional and personal satisfaction from proving that he was as good in action as on the staff. In 1942 he was delighted to be appointed in command of the destroyer *Opportune*, which was part of the escort for the Arctic convoys PQ18 and QP14, both of which suffered many attacks and losses from U-boats and the Luftwaffe. Power therefore had mixed feelings when his old chief Cunningham asked for him to be returned to his staff in September, 1942, for the planning of the TORCH landings in North Africa, to take place in November. He was awarded a CBE for his part in those operations. He stayed on the staff of Sir John Cunningham, the new C-in-C Mediterranean, for the planning of the landings in Italy, including Anzio. He was promoted Captain in December, 1943, awarded the US Legion of Merit, and twice Mentioned in Despatches.

In March, 1944, Captain Power became Captain (D) of the 26th Flotilla, his flotilla leader being *Kempenfelt*. He commanded her during the Normandy landings and in several actions against

German E-boats, for which he won his first DSO. Later in the year Captain Power transferred with his staff to *Myngs* and commanded her in the action off Lyster Light, when an enemy convoy was destroyed off the Norwegian coast in November, 1944. At the end of the year Captain Power transferred again, to *Saumarez*, which was better equipped for service in the East (where the 26th DF was due to go). Captain Peter Cazalet and his staff moved to *Myngs*.

In December, 1944, Captain and Mrs Power entertained the captains of the flotilla and their wives to dinner at the Savoy Hotel in London. It was the beginning of a happy and successful relationship. Power's reputation as a brilliant staff officer and a distinguished sea captain in combat had preceded him before he joined *Saumarez*. The flotilla now found themselves under the influence of a man whom the Flotilla Anti-Submarine Officer, Lieutenant Reay Parkinson, who had served with Power since his *Kempenfelt* days called 'the greatest sea officer I ever met'. Parkinson himself did much to assist his chief by assembling and keeping together an efficient Operations Room staff, in spite of the vagaries of wartime cross-posting, drawn from all three services.

Manley Power was something of a 'loner', who had dedicated his life to the Service. The Navy was his career, his work, his main interest, his hobby, his obsession. He very seldom relaxed and in mixed company people found him difficult to talk to. His nickname was 'Lofty', because of his manner as well as his height. He was six feet five inches tall and as his First Lieutenant in *Saumarez*, Tony Tyers, said, 'he looked down sphinx-like from his height and dominated'. Lofty Power loved action, loved the business of being at war. He was not a bully or a dictator, but he set high standards for himself and bore down cruelly on others. His officers all respected and admired him enormously, though few could claim that they ever got to know him. His personality, according to Parkinson, 'was and I expect still is, overwhelming, and his acute understanding was a mixture of Nelson and Nimitz.'

His Secretary, Denis Calnan, knew Lofty Power as well as anybody and after a friendship and acquaintance of nearly forty years felt that 'many people were frightened of Lofty Power—some still are. His physical presence and impassive exterior certainly inspired respect, if not a degree of fear. This, coupled with his natural shyness, gained him a rather undeserved reputation for unapproachability—but not among his friends who quickly realized the gentleness and honesty (with some considerable charm, when he smiled) which lay behind the formidable appearance. His personal bravery during the war is legendary—and all the stories are true. I will never forget the lesson he taught his officers in 1944 during a hot exchange of intense close-range fire with German ships off Norway—he rebuked us all for ducking our heads as the flak streamed across the bridge, making it crystal clear that he expected his officers to show no fear in the face of the enemy—whether they were frightened or not. After this, and on many occasions, we were very very careful to appear to be brave—having before our eyes his own imperturbable example. He is one of the very few men I know who genuinely felt and revelled in the joy of battle; the hotter the action the more he enjoyed it.' Typically, Power said that he did not recollect 'flak streaming across the bridge' in that action, which was 'a very one-sided and rather brutal bit of butchery'.

Saumarez' ship's company had been at action stations since 10 am and were to remain closed up, or at first state of readiness, for a total of 16 hours. At action stations Power wore full anti-flash gear, of white hood, white gloves and insisted that everybody else wear it all times in action, no matter what the heat or discomfort. Now he stood on *Saumarez*' bridge, a massive figure in his white overalls, his tin helmet in a rack close at hand, his binoculars on a leather strap round his neck. Nobody looking at his imperturbable figure, leaning with one huge forearm resting on the bridge rail, could guess that Power was about to lead his team into one of the most hazardous interceptions of the whole war.

Throughout the afternoon of the 15th, as the flotilla made a steady 27 knots to the eastward, reports were received from the Avengers and the Liberators. Positions given, and bearings of transmissions, were all plotted on *Saumarez*' chart, but their positions conflicted. At 1 pm the best estimate was that *Haguro* was within 40 miles of where Fuller had first sighted her, some 85 miles south-west of the southernmost point of Phuket Island, and still making between 10 and 20 knots in a generally south-easterly direction.

Power now paused to think over the situation. The enemy might go to Penang. If he did, the flotilla had almost no chance of catching him. He would have to be left to the aircraft in the morning. But he might, and probably would, be making for Singapore. At no time had his speed been reported at more than 20 knots, possibly because of the destroyer's fuel state. He had apparently abandoned *Kurishoyo* Maru and her escort (that is, if he had any intention of escorting them at all) and was steaming east probably to open the range from the carriers, and lessen the risk of another air attack before dark. This made sense. If Power were in that Japanese captain's place, he would have done the same: continue to open the range to eastward until after dark, then turn south and make for home at best speed.

There were other possibilities. The enemy might turn back to the north-west. If he did, *Richelieu* and *Cumberland* should be able to take care of him, although they were still miles in the rear. Captain Power also had to consider his own fuel situation. He could not exceed 27 knots for very much longer. The one advantage he did hold was that the enemy so far had no idea of the destroyers' presence. The enemy would still believe the way was clear to Singapore. As Power wrote just after the event, and repeated in conversation often in after years, his appreciation seemed 'complicated and sagacious on paper' but in fact, 'owing to the geographical configuration, it amounted to little more than the old motto of the rugger field "Go for the corner flag!".'
Power decided to carry on at 110° at 27 knots until the coast

south of Penang was reached, and then, if no enemy contact had been made, to sweep back westwards across the Malacca Strait. Later in the night, Power decided that if a second leg of the sweep was necessary, it would have to be south-westward.

Power had already decided that, unless he were obliged to, he would not attack by day, and risk the probability of the flotilla being destroyed in detail by the enemy's powerful gun armament in good visibility. If they met the enemy by day, the destroyers would try to hold the range open, keep to the southward and endeavour to lure the enemy back to the west towards *Richelieu* and *Cumberland*. (These two ships were now steaming at full stretch. Although *Cumberland*, like many of the East Indies Fleet ships, had been many months out of dock and was in any case a middle-aged lady, she could, like *Warspite* once did for Cunningham, lift her skirts and run when she put her mind to it. She was one of a famous, long-range class of ocean-going cruisers with a high speed. When Captain Du Vignaux, in *Richelieu*, asked *Cumberland* 'What speed are you making?', Captain Enwright, a man with a somewhat mischievous sense of humour, replied 'Can't hold her back at 30½ knots!')

At this time Captain Power's only real anxiety (apart from the ghastly possibility of not finding the enemy at all) 'was the danger of finding him too soon. The visibility was extreme, and I felt that our chances in daylight would be poor. There appeared for some time a possibility that we might contact him in the vicinity of Diamond Point just at or before sunset with the flotilla silhouetted against the afterglow.

'I felt that we probably just had the legs of her, as she was long out of dock. Much depended on the bearing on which she was sighted, but my intentions were, vaguely, to tease her with the 52nd (Northern) Division and work the 51st round to the South and East of her, and by feinting and using smoke to chivvy her back to the north and west. The object being, by cat and mouse tactics, to delay her until dark or until CS5 could come up. Only I was not sure which side would turn out to be the cat.'

At 3.13 pm Power signalled the flotilla that he intended a night attack, using the single ship 'star attack'—a method that *Venus* and three of the flotilla had actually practised a few nights before (and which Douglas Bromley said that 'they had exercised almost *ad nauseam*'). By this method, the destroyers would attack in their own sectors from different point of the compass; thus they would not get in each other's way, and would present a widely dispersed target themselves. Also, Power guessed that the enemy would be reluctant to turn away to the north. This constant tendency to try and make to the southward would help the enemy into the destroyer's attacking pattern.

More aircraft reports came in during the afternoon but nothing transpired to cause Captain Power to change his appreciation or his plans. At 4.40 the flotilla heard Crompton's report of his attack and his claim of possible hits. Four minutes later Power ordered his ships to form a line of bearing 295°–115°, ships four miles apart in the sequence from west to east, *Venus*, *Virago*, *Saumarez*, *Verulam* and *Vigilant*. The ships were already doing 27 knots and changes of station would take time. But Power cheerfully advised those ships that had to gain station on him, 'Don't bust yourselves'. They were all able to shake out into their stations slowly and in good time before nightfall.

From analysis of enemy sighting reports, *Saumarez'* plot estimated that the enemy's position at 7 pm that evening would be about 75 miles to the north-east of the flotilla. At 7 pm *Saumarez* herself had Diamond Point 20 miles abeam to starboard, with course still 110°, speed still 27 knots. Captain Power guessed that the enemy would probably come round to a course between 120° and 160° shortly after dark and increase speed to 20 knots. The flotilla's line of bearing was changed to 140°–320° at 7.30.

As night fell the weather turned appropriately Wagnerian. The day had been fine with slight cloud, excellent visibility and a light following wind. From dusk onwards the sky ahead of the flotilla showed flashes of lightning on great banks of cloud. Heavy rain squalls drummed down on the upper decks and periodically reduced visibility to a few hundred yards.

But the darker it got, the more confident Captain Power became. 'Once darkness fell it only remained to find him; I had no doubt as to the result. It was a flotilla party, and I felt that we all knew each other's form and that no confusion or lack of understanding could arise.' Or, as Lieutenant Calnan succinctly put it, 'If we met her at night—it was quite simple: we were to sink her.'

[5]

2245/15–0209/16 MAY

THE ATTACK

WHO WAS THIS ENEMY Captain Power and his destroyers were
hurrying to intercept? His Imperial Japanese Majesty's Ship
Haguro was a *Nachi* Class heavy cruiser, designed by Vice-Admiral
Yuzura Hiraga in accordance with the 1921 Washington Treaty
and built under the 1923 Japanese 'New Reinforcement Plan'.
The fourth and last of her class, her keel was laid down at the
Mitsubishi Yard in Nagasaki on 16 March, 1925; she was launched
on 24 March, 1928 and completed on 25 April, 1929. She had been
built, making use of lightweight materials, to comply with the
Treaty 10,000-ton limitation but her completed displacement was
actually 10,940 tons and with a full outfit of stores, oil fuel and
ammunition, she displaced some 15,000 tons—more than twice
as much as all five of her destroyer opponents put together.
Against the destroyers' four 4·7-inch guns each, in single gun
turrets, *Haguro* mounted ten 8-inch, in five turrets, the centre
turret of the forward three being mounted above the other two;
these guns, improved models of the original 8-inch, had been
installed during a year-long refit which ended on 28 December,
1939, and were capable of firing a 275 lb shell to a range of
31,600 yards (nearly sixteen miles) with a maximum rate of fire of
four rounds/minute. Her secondary armament was eight 5-inch guns
in sided twin turrets, firing a 51 lb shell to a range of 16,200 yards
with a maximum rate of fire of eight rounds/minute. In 1936
Haguro had had important structural alterations, with rebuilt
anti-torpedo bulge and an increased weight of side armour plating,

up to 5 inches thick. She had originally been fitted with four quadruple tubes, firing the formidable 'Long Lance' Type '93' oxygen-powered torpedo, carrying half a ton of explosive for eleven miles at 49 knots. In 1944, two of these torpedo tubes were removed to make way for increased anti-aircraft weapons and by May, 1945, *Haguro* mounted four triple, eight twin and twenty-four single 25 mm guns. She also had two deck catapults and was capable of carrying four seaplanes. She had two seaplanes on board that night.

Haguro was designed to make 33 knots but she was long out of dock and as Power said, he probably did have the legs of her—but only just. She had a Type 13 Air Warning radar set mounted on the main mast; operating on the 2 metre wavelength, it had a range of 31 miles, the scan being hand-rotated, with a beam 3° wide, but it had little close-range accuracy. A more modern Type 21 Air Warning Set was mounted on the foremast operating on the 1·5 metre wavelength; this had a range of over 40 miles, was power-rotated, with a beam 1·5° in width. It could theoretically pick up surface ships at about 12 miles range. The Type 22 gunnery 10 centimetre radar sets, on the port and starboard sides of the upper bridge, had a pencil beam of 0·5°, gave accurate ranges up to 15 miles for large targets, but would probably not detect Power's destroyers at much over ten miles. All these additions to armament and radar had increased the cruiser's complement to 773 in May, 1945. With a length of 661 feet, a beam of 68 feet and drawing over 20 feet, *Haguro* was much bigger, much more heavily armed and far more heavily armoured than her attackers, and just as fast.

She was also just as experienced. *Haguro* had as long and as distinguished a war history as any ship on either side. She had been one of the most faithful workhorses of the Japanese Navy and had followed the sound of guns since the opening moves. With her sister ship *Nachi* she had given seaborne cover to the Japanese invasion of Ambon on 31 January, 1942. With *Nachi* again, she was part of Admiral Takagi's Eastern Force in the

Java Sea and was in action against *Houston* and *Exeter* on 27 February, scoring at least one hit on *Exeter* and assisting in the destruction of the Dutch cruiser *De Ruyter*. At Midway she was in Takagi's 5th Cruiser Division with another sister ship *Myoko* in the Midway Covering Group of the Occupation Force; on 12 June she was detached with *Myoko* and the fleet carrier *Zuikaku* to join Admiral Hosogaya's force off the Aleutians. She took part in the defence of the Solomons, and notably in the Battle of Empress Augusta Bay on 2 November, 1943, when she and *Myoko* formed Admiral Sentoro Omori's 5th Cruiser Division. At 1.30 am that morning *Haguro* was hit by a bomb from an Allied aircraft, which opened up some side plating and caused her to reduce speed. In the subsequent action against the American cruisers under Admiral Merrill *Haguro* suffered six 6-inch shell hits but three of them were 'duds'.

Admiral Koga assigned *Haguro* and *Myoko* to Kawase's command at Paramushiro when the Americans attacked Attu in the Aleutians in May, 1943. When the war was going against the Japanese 18th Army in New Guinea in 1944, *Haguro* and *Myoko* with the battleship *Fuso* were part of the screening force for the KON plan to transport 2,500 troops of the Japanese 2nd Amphibious Brigade from Mindanao to Biak in May. The next month *Haguro* and *Myoko* were part of the Attack Force with the giant battleships *Yamato* and *Mussashi* which hastened north from Batjan under Rear-Admiral Matome Ugaki to rendezvous with Admiral Ozawa in the Philippine Sea. *Haguro* and *Myoko* then formed the 5th Cruiser Division again, under Rear-Admiral Shintaro Hashimoto, in the great battle that followed.

When Ozawa's flagship the new carrier *Taiho* was torpedoed and sunk on 19 June, it was to *Haguro* that the fleet commander, his staff and the Emperor's portrait were transferred from the destroyer *Wakasuki* by lifeboat during the afternoon. It was in a small cabin under *Haguro*'s bridge, jammed with his own staff, and with the cruiser's limited signalling equipment, that the Admiral struggled to regain control of his fleet. *Haguro* straggled from the rest of the ships during the night, and no doubt it was a relief to everybody when Ozawa was at last able to transfer to the big fleet carrier *Zuikaku* at 1 pm the next day. Later, in the evening, *Haguro* was ordered with Admiral Kurita and the entire Japanese van to steam eastward and seek a night action. But the order was cancelled and *Haguro* survived to be part of Kurita's Centre Force in the climactic naval battle of Leyte Gulf.

With Captain Kaju Sugiura, who commanded her on her last sortie, and many of the same officers and ship's company on board, *Haguro* was one of the force of heavy cruisers who emerged unmolested with Kurita through the San Bernardino Strait early on the morning of 25 October. For a time they unknowingly had the troop anchorage of Leyte at their mercy. Despite persistent attacks by US destroyers, *Haguro* and the other heavy cruisers came the closest of all to the Allied fleet before Kurita, mistaking Admiral Sprague's escort carriers for Mitscher's fleet carriers, and the destroyers and transports he could see for Halsey's Third Fleet, ordered a general retirement. After the battle *Haguro* had gone to Singapore where, with another sister ship, *Ashigara*, she formed the 5th Cruiser Squadron under Rear-Admiral Hashimoto. By May, 1945, like the men in most of the larger Japanese warships, *Haguro*'s ship's company probably lacked a little sea-time, but *Haguro* was still a big, fast, heavily armed and experienced enemy. Such a wily old campaigner was not likely to be caught easily and Power's destroyers would need luck (some of which they had already had) and some Japanese errors if they were to sink her.

At dusk the destroyers had darkened ship as usual. Scuttle deadlights were screwed down, black muslin screens were hung in folds by upper deck doors, only the dimmest red lighting was allowed on the instruments in the Action Information Centre. The rigid black-out served to intensify the sense of isolation of the men at their action stations. In the sticky heat below, men were left to their own thoughts, with occasional broadcast messages over the ship's loudspeakers, augmented by the inevitable word of mouth 'buzzes'. 'Just got the buzz, the Avengers got her this afternoon. She's sunk!' The news aroused wild surges of hope in the listeners. Perhaps there would be no need for them to go into action after all! But the ship was still rattling on at the same speed. Nothing had changed.

As the hours passed, everybody gradually accepted that he was being carried into battle, willy-nilly, whether he liked it or not. Captain (D) on the bridge, a man they all had seen and heard but few of them had met, was taking them all where he wanted them to go, and the best way to take it was to accept it. 'I won't say the ship was agog with excitement,' said Stoker Petty Officer 'Spud' Yates, in *Saumarez*, 'because by that time most of the crew were hardened veterans, the majority of the same crowd having served in *Saumarez* during the *Scharnhorst* battle. At ten o'clock Chief Stoker Cadwallader came into the PO's Mess and told the watch going below for the Middle that anti-flash gear and gloves were to be worn by all. He threatened castration and other diabolical tortures to any man found disobeying these orders—a precaution which in due course proved to be the best possible advice for us.'

Since 10 pm the ship's companies had been at a relaxed state of Action Stations, where men were allowed to leave their posts to get and take food up to those on watch. To most the food was welcome. 'I can still remember the taste and feel of bully beef,' wrote Lieutenant Calnan, 'tepid from a sunwarmed can, eaten with the fingers, and washed down with tinned apricots, fruit and juice and all running stickily down my chin.'

But the food did not agree with everybody. In *Venus'* Action Information Centre, Ordinary Seaman Norman Poole, on watch on the 293 Radar Set, was feeling uncomfortably queasy. His stomach was rebelling at the dinner of 'a mess of spuds, another veg and "cold dog"' which had already made him violently sick during the first dogwatch that evening. At their relaxed action stations, only communications numbers were closed up, while everybody else took the chance to get some rest, so Poole was alone on 293 watch, his fellow watchkeepers, Ordinary Seaman

113

Paddy Brien and 'Smitty' Smith being asleep on the deck of the flat outside the Captain's cabin, one deck below the AIC.

The 293 PPI screen had been showing the smudges and blotches of rain-squall echoes all evening. At 10.40 Poole was plotting one particular squall when he noticed, inside the spreading main echo, the hard bright dot of a solid target. He tried to plot it, but at that extreme range, values were only guesses.

'Bridge . . . Plot.' Poole's voice crackled over the broadcast.

'Bridge?'

'This is Plot, sir. Is there any land bearing zero-four-five?'

'Negative. The nearest land on that bearing is Burma. Looks like a squall!'

'Plot, roger.'

Poole carried on plotting the target echo. There was no doubt, it was a good solid target. At 10.50 he reported to the bridge again.

'Bridge . . . Plot, I have a good solid echo on that bearing, sir. Bearing zero-four-five, range sixty-eight thousand yards, sir.'

There was a pause, and Poole knew what they were thinking on the bridge. Sixty-eight thousand yards, or thirty-four miles, was well outside the normal range of the 293 set.

'Plot . . . Bridge. Investigate.'

'Plot, roger.'

At 11 pm Poole made another report. 'Echo zero-four-three, range fifty-four thousand yards.'

At last the bridge awoke to the possibility of a real target and in Poole's own words, 'there was *panic*'. The broadcast speaker reverberated with requests for ranges, bearings, speeds and courses. Overwhelmed, Poole turned in his seat and asked the first person he saw, who happened to be the Chief Torpedo Instructor, to go down and shake his two fellow-watchkeepers below. It seemed to Poole an age before they appeared and all the while the bridge was clamouring for more information. At 11.02 the bearing was 042°, range still 54,000 yards.

When Brien and Smith arrived in the AIC they were accompanied by the Leading Radar Operator and the Radar Mechanician, who were both sceptical of Poole's contact because there was no corresponding echo on the main set PPI. Poole was pushed protesting aside, while his seniors adjusted his set. The echo promptly vanished, at 11.04. Poole exchanged some hot and hard words with the leading hand, but then, realizing what he had said, he said no more. But he did succeed in getting his seat back. No sooner had he readjusted his set than it recognized 'his master's touch' on the knobs and the echo reappeared, at 11.10. The bearing was now 039°, range 53,000 yards. If this was a cloud, then it was behaving in a most remarkably purposeful manner.

The contact was confirmed as a surface echo by the Radar Officer, Lieutenant Paxton, RCNVR at 11.11. From 11.15 onwards the echo's progress was reported every minute. At twenty past, Poole was able to give a course and speed.

'Course one-three-five, speed two-five, sir . . .'

Commander de Chair now allocated the contact a genuine echo code number 'Jig 541' and at 11.22 made by TBS to *Saumarez* the first enemy report:

Venus to D.26, Jig five-four-one zero-four-zero (bearing), two-three (twenty-three miles), Queen one-three-five (course) Roger two-five (speed).

Captain Power was as sceptical as de Chair had been and at once replied:

'Interrogative Jig five-four-one Popeye' which meant 'Question whether your Jig might be a cloud (Popeye).'

De Chair replied that he did not think it was a cloud and at 11.32 the Plot reported that the Jig appeared to be altering to starboard. At 11.38, *Venus* passed the new target course, one-seven-zero: nearly due south, and steering even closer to the flotilla. Just as Power had forecast, the enemy was now heading directly for Singapore after sunset, with no idea that destroyers might be between them and home.

There was still no corresponding echo on any other radar set in the flotilla, but at 11.45 Captain Power allocated the destroyers their lettered sectors for a 'star' attack and signalled an enemy sighting report to Colombo. Three minutes later the echo faded from *Venus'* screen. The same meteorological phenomenon which had betrayed *Haguro* by extending *Venus'* radar range now helped to shield her. *Venus'* scan had been stopped and locked on *Haguro's* bearing, being trained fractions of a degree as necessary by hand, to give continuous readings of the target. The full sweep was started again, but the strip of light sweeping round and round on the orange surface now showed nothing but the rainclouds and the flotilla. *Haguro* had disappeared as completely as though she had dived like a submarine. At 11.55 Captain Power ordered *Venus* to close her target. He now had no doubt that this *was* the target and Ordinary Seaman Poole, who had had the courage of his convictions in de Chair's words 'almost to the point of insubordination', had been completely vindicated.

As *Venus* swung away to head for her target, *Saumarez* also picked up the echo for the first time, at three minutes after midnight. The bearing was 010°, range 14 miles. Power was resting briefly in his sea cabin, heard the report over the broadcast and went down to the Action Information Centre (AIC) to study the plot. Comparison with *Venus'* plot showed that this was their target too. The contact plots coincided almost exactly. A minute later, *Venus* had 'her' echo again—bearing 035°, range 35,500 yards.

When *Venus* lost her contact, Power turned his destroyers due northwards, speed 20 knots, to close the target. Although he had already located sectors and sent off an enemy report, he was still not certain of their target's intentions. To spread the flotilla between the enemy and the coast, and to put it in a position to encircle him from the south-west, Power ordered the 51st Division, of *Vigilant* and *Verulam*, to form on a line of bearing 070° from *Saumarez*. After a few minutes Power saw *Virago* edging in too close for his comfort to *Saumarez'* port quarter and ordered her to steer more to the westward to equalize the gap that had appeared between *Saumarez* and *Venus*.

As soon as *Saumarez* had the contact on radar, Power turned his ships together due south and reduced speed to 12 knots, to allow the enemy to catch up, and to give the destroyers a better chance of reaching their attacking sectors around the enemy. It was, in fact, just like laying a net in front of an advancing quarry and waiting for him to rush into it.

Now that *Saumarez* also had the contact on her radar screen, Captain Power could look at the whole situation as it developed on the Plot in *Saumarez'* AIC. The small, dimly red-lit compartment was packed with men, radar screens, instruments, telephones, voice-pipes and equipment, and dominated by the main Plot in the centre. It was uncomfortably hot at Action Stations, with barely room to move about. Besides Captain Power himself, there was the Flotilla Navigating Officer, Lieutenant C. H. H. Knollys, as Plotting Officer; Lieutenant Reay Parkinson; Lieutenant M. Marwood, the Communications Officer; Lieutenant D. Stobie, the Flotilla Torpedo Officer; Sub-Lieutenant (SP) J. P. Gardiner, the Action Cypher Officer; Writer Alan Parsons, keeping the Action Narrative; a Leading Seaman as Principal Plotter, and other seamen and radar plotters, manning telephones to the bridge, to the torpedo tubes and the bridge sights; another torpedo rating on the firing panel, plus many sailors for target indication, gun liaison operators, communications numbers in constant touch with the Gun Control Director, the Transmitting Station and the Principal Control Officers. It was a hubbub of commands and reports, no matter how hard Captain Power and Parkinson tried to keep the noise level down.

Power, with Parkinson and Knollys, had chosen their own AIC teams and managed to keep them together, so that they understood and trusted each other. They had redesigned the lay-out of the AIC compartment and the positioning of the various speakers, recorders, displays and tables. They had practised it all more times than they could remember, rehearsed it and rehearsed it again until they could all recite their parts by rote. Now they were, they hoped, just about to see the results of all their preparations and hard work. Most of the AIC ratings were 'hostilities only'

117

men, absorbed in their own immediate duties. But Power, Parkinson, Stobie, Knollys and Marwood were all regular RN officers and even at the height of the action could still preserve a residue of professional detachment. Whatever happened, they would still be professionally curious to see whether their theories worked in practice. Had they done the drills the right way and, if not, how should they be changed?

Also in the AIC throughout the action were the ship's mascots, Minnie the cat and an Alsatian pup called Punch. 'They were both quite unperturbed by the noise,' Knollys told the *Times of Ceylon* afterwards, 'as they are well accustomed to action by now. Minnie was marking the positions on the chart with her paw regularly every four minutes.'

Lieutenant Calnan has left a description of *Saumarez*' officers as the ship went into battle. 'The Operations Room crew—silent, strained and apprehensive: the bridge crew much happier—out in the open where a man is much braver, but still strained and jumpy. My Captain, massively imperturbable as ever, standing on the compass platform with one enormous arm resting on top of the pelorus, a giant figure in white overalls, anti-flash gloves and hood, silent too—but grinning with joyful anticipation like a naughty boy. He indeed had the joy of battle to come strong in him, and his example was contagious—to some of us. I do believe that only three of us felt—or outwardly showed—that indescribable exhilaration of the prospect of action: my Captain, Reay Parkinson, smiling like a black Cheshire Cat, devil's eyebrows hooked like a clown's leaning like a fat sack over the chart table in the operations room, purring with satisfaction as he watched his plot develop. I myself was just plain over-excited. But the others—terribly British and very brave—pretending to be un-emotional, calm and faintly bored. I could not understand their attitude, then or now.'

Events began now to slot into place, as Power and his flotilla officers had always hoped and dreamed. At 12.07 the enemy's course was estimated at 170°, probably zigzagging, speed 20

11 *Saumarez*: Action Information Centre with (*left*) Plotting Officer and Principal Plotter; in background, Flotilla Anti-submarine Officer, and Able-Seaman on Target Indication, Torpedo Firing and Radar Plotting.

12 *Saumarez*: Action Information Centre with Plotting Officer and Principal Plotter at the table. Action Narrative Writer and Action Cypher Officer in the background.

13 *Saumarez*: Action Information Centre–Blind Torpedo Firing Arrangements. *Left*, Torpedo Firing Officer; *right*, Plotting Officer and Principal Plotter.

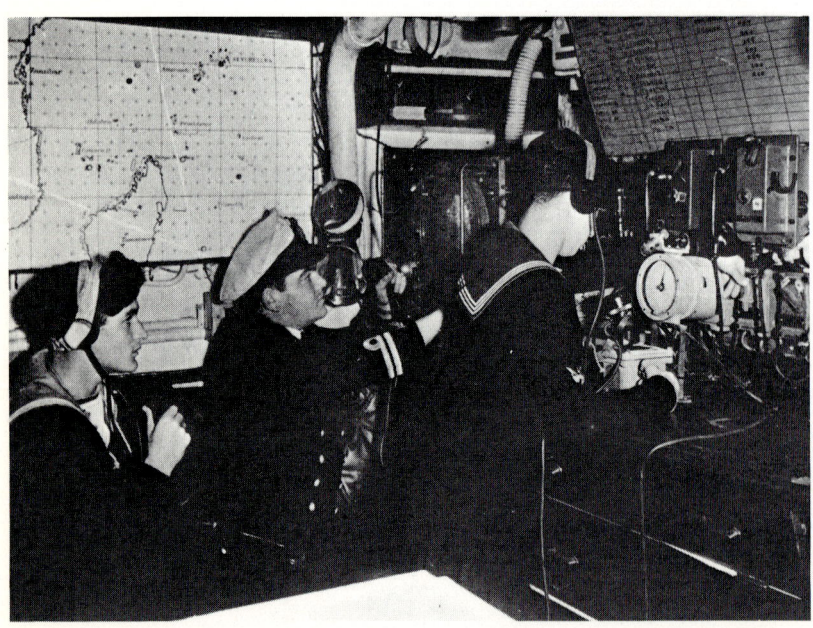

14 *Saumarez*: Action Information Centre–Target Indication and Gun Liaison. *Left*, Gun Liaison Operator; *centre*, Anti-submarine Officer; *right*, Interlinking Unit Operator.

knots, and all five destroyers were steaming in front of her, waiting for her to catch up. At 12.15, when the range was thirteen miles, the flotilla altered course back to north. As they closed, the 'radar scans at this time presented a picture which would have been approved by Medina Sidonia—the flotilla bearing down on the enemy in a deep crescent with the tips of the horns about to complete his encirclement'.

Venus' various manœuvres had left her to the northward of the rest and at 12.25 Captain Power allocated new attacking sectors, giving *Venus* Sector George, to the north-west. At 12.39 he signalled to the flotilla that he intended to attack at 1 am. This gave the others a datum time at which to try and co-ordinate their own attacks. Captain Power ordered the torpedoes to be set to run at a mean depth of 9 feet, so that they could also hit the enemy destroyer (and also, of course, Power's own destroyers, if attacks should become unco-ordinated). The destroyer had not yet actually been detected, but Power was assuming she had still stayed in company since the last aircraft sighting.

One by one the other destroyers, *Verulam* at 12.25, then *Virago*, and finally *Vigilant* whose radar set had been giving trouble, at 12.35, picked up the target, and *Venus* was at last able to discontinue transmitting enemy reports. It was nearly two hours since Norman Poole had picked up that first incredible, faintly scoffed-at target echo, and he had been tracking ever since. He well deserved the DSM he was awarded after the action.

At about 12.45, when the enemy's range had come down to ten miles, he seemed suddenly to become aware of possible danger and swung away first to the west and then, manœuvring freely, back towards his mean course of about 170°. Shortly afterwards, at a range of nine miles, the target echo split and a second, much smaller, echo could be seen close astern of the first. This was *Kamikaze*, a venerable little destroyer, of 1,400 tons, launched in September, 1922, and now commanded by Lieutenant-Commander Kinichi Kasuga; originally she had had a speed of some 37 knots and could still make 34 in May, 1945. She was armed with three

4·7-inch guns in single turrets, thirteen 25 mm and three single 13 mm anti-aircraft guns. She also carried eighteen depth-charges. Three twin torpedo tubes, originally fitted, had been removed in 1945, possibly to make room for increased AA armament.

It seemed very probable that *Haguro*'s radar had picked up echoes ahead at that range of about ten miles. Sugiura would not expect danger from the south from surface ships. The echo or echoes would probably have been classified as surfaced submarines and the free manœuvring might well have been an exaggerated anti-submarine zigzag around a mean course of south.

At 12.49 Captain Power signalled *Venus* and *Virago* to 'close the enemy' and both ships went to 'Full Ahead' together. *Saumarez* herself was still well placed for her own attack which Power intended to be from the enemy's starboard bow. The enemy's course was now about 160°. *Saumarez* altered to close the enemy as well at 20 knots, and at a range of about six miles Power left the Plot and went up to the bridge. As he said, 'The timing of the move from Plot to bridge is always a subject of controversy. This one turned out right, because although I did miss personal observation of important tactical developments in the Plot I had time to settle down comfortably on the bridge before the action developed'. At 12.50, Power felt that 'the situation was entirely in accordance with plan. The net was spread and the quarry, with little encouragement was walking straight into it.'

But it was all a little too perfect to be true. Only four minutes after Captain Power was experiencing such satisfied feelings, *Haguro* turned right round to starboard and, obviously now thoroughly alarmed, set off to the north-west, increasing speed as she went. *Kamikaze* made a wide sweep out to the east and then turned sharply back to the west towards *Haguro*'s starboard quarter. Power's carefully laid plans for a nice, calculated bow shot were ruined.

As soon as the Plot reported the enemy's change of course, Power ordered full ahead and began to chase after his enemy at 30 knots. He later reproached himself for the delay, feeling that he should himself have noticed sooner that the range had stopped coming down and begun to open again. At that time radar operators did not amplify their reports with any words such as 'closing', 'opening' or 'steady'. A captain listening to a monotonous stream of radar reports, without acknowledging each one, tended to get semi-hypnotized by the operator's voice.

At any rate, Power now found himself with a high speed stern chase, and, in what he called a moment of irritation, he signalled the flotilla: 'Am unable to attack now', which, he said afterwards, 'was an extremely silly signal to make. It could be no conceivable use to anyone and could only, and in fact did, cause confusion in the minds of some Commanding Officers'.

Haguro had indeed detected the 26th Destroyer Flotilla at about the time she was seen on the destroyers' radar screens to make a violent alteration of course to the west. From 5 pm onwards that afternoon *Haguro* had been receiving urgent reports from Sabang and Sumatra, 'Many cruisers and destroyers in sight', and 'Many ships including aircraft carriers and battleships rushing into Malacca Strait'. At dusk, Rear-Admiral Hashimoto, the 5th Cruiser Squadron commander, who was on board, ordered Captain Sugiura to make for the Malacca Strait, just as Power had forecast she probably would. *Haguro* was fast enough to outrun pursuit, given her head start, and would certainly have done so, but for the caution of her Navigating Officer, Commander Ota. He was new to the ship, having only just joined before she left Singapore; possibly he was new to the Malacca Strait as well. With the lack of navigational aids in the Strait, he was not confident enough of avoiding the Japanese minefields off Singapore by night and preferred to arrive after dawn. Thus *Haguro*'s speed was reduced to 24 knots until midnight, and 21 knots thereafter. This, unfortunately for *Haguro*, gave Power's destroyers the leeway to catch up. Hashimoto and Sugiura agreed with Ota and signalled their intentions ahead to Singapore. They did not ask for air cover, knowing (significantly) that it would not be forthcoming.

It was curious how both sides weighed the same factors and reached roughly the same conclusions. Hashimoto, Sugiura and their staffs estimated, quite correctly, that any pursuing force would catch up at about 1 am on 16 May. But they hoped that the pursuing ships might turn back at midnight, having by then sighted nothing and knowing that if they carried on they might find themselves too close to the coast of Malaya at dawn.

On passage down to the Malacca Strait *Haguro*'s ship's company were in three watches with a third of the crew on watch at a time, and the rest stood down. Very few of *Haguro*'s officers survived the action. One account of the last hours on her bridge is from Lieutenant-Commander Isamu Motora, a communications officer whose action station was on the bridge, assisting the Captain. Motora was sound asleep on his bunk at the rear of the bridge when the alarm was sounded at 12.50 am. Motora rushed to the bridge and found Admiral Hashimoto and Captain Sugiura already there, staring ahead through their binoculars. The officer of the watch was just leaving the bridge to go to his own action station, the Captain having taken control of the ship.

According to Motora's account, that officer of the watch had been guilty of gross negligence. He was a veteran on board, having been in *Haguro* for more than two years, but had failed to warn the captain until far too late. *Haguro*'s radar had detected the enemy destroyers at 20,000 metres range, or over ten miles. Bridge lookouts had reported the destroyers in sight at 18,000 metres, or more than nine miles (the Japanese had demonstrated their truly superb night vision in dozens of actions in the Pacific sea war). But, according to Motora, the officer of the watch had taken no action and when Motora joined his senior officers at the front of the bridge, he was horrified and dumbfounded to see, as they could, four destroyers strung out in a line in front of *Haguro*, and only just 6,000 metres away (*Venus*, the fifth, was then astern, on *Haguro*'s starboard quarter). The destroyers were to the south-west and south-east of *Haguro* and between her and Singapore. *Haguro* had run right into the trap.

After a moment's staggered silence, Sugiura ordered the helm hard-a-starboard and gave the order for the main armament to open fire on the port-hand destroyer. Hashimoto now ordered Sugiura to head for Penang (exactly the outcome Commodore Searle had foreseen), but first they would have to deal with the destroyers.

Haguro's dash to the north took her towards *Venus*, who had been astern of her. Suddenly, de Chair could see the cruiser silhouetted by lightning, closing rapidly, moving right. Radar had also picked up *Kamikaze* abeam of *Haguro*. De Chair planned to pass between *Haguro* and the destroyer and attack from *Haguro*'s starboard bow. Tubes were brought to the ready and at 1.06 am de Chair signalled 'Attacking'.

'The First Lieutenant, as Gunnery Control Officer, was on the bridge with me, and the Sub-Lieutenant was below in charge of the Plot until required to fire torpedoes from the bridge. Shortly before the time ordered to attack, he reported that the range was closing rapidly, with a small echo to the left of the big one. Clearly the cruiser had spotted our destroyers ahead, turned round and was coming towards us at a relative speed of about 60 knots with a destroyer on her starboard beam. I told the First Lieutenant we would aim to pass between the two ships and fire our torpedoes at the cruiser as we passed. I hoped that in the resulting confusion the two enemy ships might fire at each other.'

Meryon, the First Lieutenant, was looking at *Haguro* through his binoculars, 'She looked huge to me when we passed on opposite courses. I recall that we were a good deal closer than the 4,000 yards referred to in later reports because I am certain I had a sighting of her at one stage in my 1900A binoculars and the ship took up the full width of the binocular vision. I feel sure at that point her guns were still trained fore and aft.'

Meanwhile, de Chair got ready for his attack. 'I ordered the Sub-Lieutenant to come up on the bridge and prepare to fire torpedoes, and reported 'Attacking'. We could see the cruiser ahead with night glasses and were obviously going to be in a perfect position to fire torpedoes on the beam at very close range. When nearing the firing position I said to the Torpedo Control Officer, "Are you ready, Sub?" but received no answer. By this time the enemy was very close, about 45° on our bow, her two funnels filled my glasses and I repeated, "Are you ready, Sub?" He said in a quiet voice, "We've missed it, sir." He had angled the torpedoes ahead, in spite of my order for straight running on the beam, and it was too late to alter the settings. Short of ramming the cruiser, or possibly fouling *Saumarez* or *Verulam* somewhere astern of her, I had no alternative but to turn to port, which I did under full helm, to try and prevent the Jap from breaking out of our circle. Evidently he saw us turn and, assuming we had fired torpedoes, turned away to comb the tracks. This threw him back into the arms of Captain "D" and *Verulam*.'

Haguro was now racing southwards back towards *Saumarez* again. *Saumarez'* First Lieutenant, Lieutenant Tony Tyers, was aft, at his action station in charge of the two after guns, so placed, as he told his wife in a somewhat unreassuring letter, 'so that if anything happens to the bridge team, there would be someone with a bit of experience left to get the remains home, so you can visualize me standing in a position open to all four winds with very little to hide behind!!! From the time we felt the engines increase speed, just after the announcement that we were going to attack, there was a complete silence among the guns' crews, and I think it was pretty general throughout the ship.

'I could hear over another loudspeaker the ranges and bearings of the enemy being passed to the bridge, and as the range closed, so we held our breaths, waiting for a salvo of 8-inch to come hurtling towards us; and so the range shortened, complete silence, except for the voice on the loudspeaker saying "8,000 yards, sir, 7,000 yards, sir". I wonder what everyone was thinking—but still the dramatic silence held as the ship rushed at full speed closer and closer to the enemy, who was lit up by lightning flashes, but even without those you could see the cruiser by this time as a large black blob on the horizon.'

Once again Power's attacking plan had been disrupted. His bow shot had turned to a stern chase and back to a head-on shot again, with the enemy tearing towards him at over 60 mph. Knollys could see the whole picture from the tracks on the Plot in front of him. 'It was like a net closing in,' he said, 'and we were expecting the quarry to begin snapping at any moment. In spite of the very close ranges, not a shot had been fired, and it seemed uncanny to be chasing this silent and so far invisible monster around his own backyard without once being bitten.

'Events from now on began to move pretty fast. From the bridge the enemy destroyer's bow wave was suddenly seen ahead.'

Saumarez' manœuvrings had taken her out of her proper sector, Sector 'Dog', and into *Vigilant*'s Sector 'Baker' but Power was quite oblivious of this fact. 'At the time I had forgotten all about sectors, other ships, or anything else except the urgent need to close the enemy.' Power saw *Kamikaze* ahead, saw that the two ships were converging rapidly and that *Kamikaze* was well placed to fire torpedoes. Instinctively he gave the order, 'hard-a-starboard!' to pass under the enemy destroyer's stern, and *Kamikaze* slid rapidly down *Saumarez'* port side.

Not so rapidly, however, as to get off scot-free. 'The next few moments were confused but exciting,' wrote Calnan. 'The enemy destroyer reappeared under our port bow, and as she passed close down our port side at more than fifty knots relative speed, the Bofors raked her from stem to stern.

'Above the growl and groan of the stabilized mounting, always level in spite of the heel and slew of the ship, I heard my layer yelling wordlessly as he depressed the gun and stamped on the pedal: then the shells streamed out in a hosepipe sweep, the tracers hitting along her whole length—no ricochets on this soft target.'

Kamikaze had been sighted at only 3,000 yards range but she had been tracked and held by *Saumarez'* gunnery radar, and as *Saumarez* wheeled to starboard 'A' gun (the only one able to fire, 'B' gun being loaded with starshell) opened fire under radar control, shifting to visual after two salvoes, as soon as the layer could see the approaching destroyer. As *Saumarez* turned to port again to cross *Kamikaze*'s stern 'A' gun would no longer bear, but later claimed three hits in the short time it had been in action. *Kamikaze*'s own 4·7-inch guns appeared to be still trained fore and aft as she raced past and a signal lamp could be seen flashing frantically from her upper bridge, as though astounded at this unwarranted and unfair assault.

Kamikaze at last got her guns into action, though possibly only close range weapons, as she passed off *Saumarez*' port quarter, but took no further part in the action and nobody saw her definitely again. *Haguro* was much more alert and opened with 5-inch starshell which illuminated *Saumarez* in a brilliant glow. *Saumarez* herself also opened with starshell from 'B' gun at 1.08 am. Power now got his first clear look at his enemy. 'She looked pretty big and her direction was easy to see by her bow wave and wash. Inclination vague but obviously broad. I thought she was going very fast. Her side was shining like a wet wall, with the reflection of her own starshell from behind us, I think.'

As soon as he saw her, Power realized his tubes were trained out on the wrong side, i.e. to starboard, from the previous frustrated approach. Power might have thought that 'foresight and providence should have prompted me to train the tubes to port as soon as the Plot reported the cruiser going left. To have done so would have made the shot far easier and would have exposed the ship far less'. But this would have been a policy of perfection and as there was no time to train the tubes round, Power decided to swing his whole ship round to port, 'like a shot-gun'.

'I was just considering turning to fire when our boiler got hit. There was a lot of steam and smoke amidships and a sort of queer silence. The ship was obviously slowing down and I thought she was going to stop. Enemy was still right ahead. The prime requirement being to get the torpedoes away, I went port 25 to get round before we lost way and told the Torpedo Firing Officer to stand by.

'In fact, owing to the use of the unit system, the starboard screw was still heaving round full speed, and with this and the wheel the ship slewed round very quickly. Just as the sights were coming on a very heavy shell splash arrived on the bridge, the bulk of it falling on the TFO and his sight. Before he could come up for air it was obviously time to fire, and I ordered "Fire One" by eye from the binnacle (this had been practised frequently). The rest were fired automatically by interval. The TFO surfaced in time to see the enemy crossing his centre prong at about the 3rd or 4th torpedo.

'As soon as the fish had all gone wheel was put hard over and telegraphs to "full" with a view to as quick a getaway as possible. Smoke was also made and was effective, the ship being steadied with smoke lying fine on the starboard quarter but as salvoes were still pitching close on the starboard beam I altered a little to port and looking aft along the port side, saw the cruiser hit at that time.

'The hits were very distinct—three gold coloured splashes like a Prince of Wales' feathers—more than twice as high as her bridge. She did not fire any more.'

It may have appeared to Power that *Haguro* was no longer firing, but she certainly was. Calnan and his Bofors crew were under no misapprehensions about that. 'All this time I had been conscious that the familiar crack of our 4·7s and the thump-thump-thump of my own guns were being blotted out by a gigantic hammering storm of tremendous noise, drowning all speech and sense. *Haguro* was firing on us, point-blank, with her main armament, opening with a full ten-gun broadside.

'At this moment I had forgotten her existence, and could not comprehend why great waterfalls of water were erupting before and behind me. *Haguro*'s salvoes were pitching close aboard, short and over, and the tons of water thrown up were swamping the upper deck so that our position was awash up to the lids of the ready-use lockers.'

Haguro's main armament was firing by radar control, and very accurately, with a spread of seldom more than 200 yards per salvo and a rate of fire of some 6 to 8 rounds per minute. At about 1 am an 8-inch shell glanced off *Saumarez*' forecastle nicking a twelve-inch chip out of the deck edge on the port side between 'A' gun mounting and the bridge superstructure screen. Almost immediately afterwards a 5-inch shell or possibly a 4·7-inch from *Kamikaze* hit the top of *Saumarez*' funnel and blew a section of it away. One red-hot splinter fell on Surgeon Lieutenant Mike Evans, on deck below the funnel, but another 8-inch salvo pitched close alongside and the water tumbling inboard quenched the splinter. Beside the doctor was Leading Steward Marshall, lying flat on his face on the deck. Marshall had served in Arctic convoys on the fleet minesweeper *Hussar* but nothing in his previous war service had left him as exposed as this. Lying there, he felt sharp stabs on his back and was convinced he had been riddled with splinters. When he got up he asked somebody to look at his back. They found nothing. He had been forcibly sprayed with water drops, which had felt like metal shards.

On the bridge, the noise of explosions, escaping steam and rushing water made normal conversation impossible. Tons of water crashed into the bridge space, drenching everybody there, swamping telephones and hand-sets, and cascading in torrents down on to the upper deck. It was uncomfortable, but not lethal. As Power said, 'If you are only getting wet there is nothing to worry about'.

Unfortunately, *Saumarez* was not merely getting wet. *Haguro*'s 5-inch salvoes had not been as accurate as the 8-inch but at 1.11 a 5-inch shell entered below the bridge and penetrated to the forward No 1 Boiler Room. In the AIC everything went a ghastly quiet and the compartment filled with steam. Writer Alan Parsons was trying to write up the action log. 'I quite honestly thought our last moment had come and I thought of everyone at home with the war over. What a way to finish. There was a moment of incredible silence—I just waited for the ship to blow up, steam arose, there were shouts, I think an emergency light came on and we got under way—we couldn't believe our luck.'

Parsons' sensations were shared by most in the AIC including Knollys, the Navigating Officer, 'We felt a bit of a blow and there was a rush of escaping steam. In the charthouse we felt the ship heeling over and all the lights went out. Then steam and shell fumes began to fill the air. There followed a rather eerie quiet and it felt as though we had stopped. We didn't quite know what had happened but when the lights came on again we still seemed to be the right way up. Actually, owing to heroic work by the Engine Room Staff, the ship had barely faltered in her stride.'

On deck, beside his Bofors, Calnan felt *Saumarez* heeling 'far over to starboard (beyond the maximum depression of the gun) as we slewed to port. The Bofors stopped firing, and I glimpsed the high, shining wet side of *Haguro* herself, lit by intermittent lightning flashes and our rocket flares.

'As *Saumarez* swung further to port, closing *Haguro* at thirty knots, a tremendous crack and a roar like the end of the world overwhelmed us; all our guns stopped firing.

'An unnerving silence fell: all power was off and communications dead. Deaf, wet and confused I looked forward and saw that the upper half of the funnel—thirty feet away—had disappeared. The remnant was belching out a towering eruption of steam and smoke. The silence was not silence, but the total deafness caused by the tearing shriek of escaping superheated steam. Beneath my feet the deck tilted even more to starboard as our turn to port tightened, and looking down on to the iron deck a few feet below me I saw (but could not hear) all eight torpedoes leap, one by one, from their tubes, trained to starboard.

'Slowly, *Saumarez* came upright and slowly she appeared to be coming to a halt. We were no longer under fire, our guns were silent, and the enemy had vanished. The uncanny stillness persisted; only the steam still roared out.

'I looked astern, and saw three golden explosions split the blackness. *Haguro* was hit. The time was 0115. We had been in close action exactly ten minutes.'

From the bridge Parkinson was, like the others, impressed by

Haguro's size. 'She seemed to tower above us like a skyscraper and her guns were depressed to their lowest angle.' Petty Officer L. G. Finch, who actually fired the torpedoes, saw 'a sheet of white flame which enveloped the ship from stem to stern, as well as internal fires which made her glow.'

The 5-inch shell in No 1 Boiler Room penetrated the boiler, although Stoker PO 'Spud' Yates in charge of the boiler room watch then, did not realize that at first. 'I saw what appeared to be a flash on the main steam pipe. Amazing how vivid the impression is yet. I didn't discover that the shell had actually penetrated the boiler until much later. It's a good job it did otherwise I don't think I would be writing this. Immediately steam began to fill the boiler room at a temperature of somewhere around 500°F. Leading Stoker Pincher Marten, the water-tender, was nearest the point of impact, being on the gratings practically level with the top of the boiler. Leading Stoker Ginger Elliott was watch-keeper on the diesel generator (always running at action stations) which was on the port side of the boiler room, the side where the shell penetrated. He, poor devil, received the full blast of the escaping steam. I should imagine he died instantly. Stoker Daniel Hendren was on the plates, as I was.

'The very first thing that came into my head was to keep the steam away from us. The only way to do this was to open wide the throttle to the fans supplying forced draught air to the boiler room. This I did and at the same time shouted a warning to the others. Naval procedure would have been for me to say, "Evacuate the boiler room" but I just shouted, "Look out!" Marten understood and made rapidly for the emergency hatch on the starboard side of the boiler room deck-head. Elliott was slumped in a corner by the diesel and Hendren was on his knees on the plates, the steam already beginning to choke him. I was lucky, being directly under the intake of air from the fan. It would have been impossible for me to carry either Elliott or Hendren out of the boiler room as both were pretty hefty lads and the ladders leading upwards to the deck were far too steep. It was a case of getting away from the deadly searing steam in order to breathe and this I did. The thought of fire then crossed my mind and I went to the secondary position in the fan flat (above the boiler room) and shut down the steam supply to the oil fuel pump and heaters. I then reported to damage control who then informed the bridge that No 1 Boiler Room was out of action. We couldn't raise the engine room on the telephone so I went back amidships and informed Commander (E) Robins personally. I remember how hot the deck plates over the boiler room were, because somewhere along the line I had lost my shoes and was walking in my stockinged feet.'

Haguro's preoccupation with *Saumarez* had allowed *Verulam* to run in and make her attack unobserved, and without a finger laid on her. At first Douglas Bromley had thought he was closing too fast and had altered course out to the eastward. When Power signalled that he could not attack at 1 am Bromley was given more time to gain position. By 1.03 *Verulam* was closing her target again at a relative speed of over 50 knots. *Haguro* was actually sighted at about 1.09, range 8,000 yards, bearing Green (starboard) 30, inclination about 150 degrees left. *Verulam*'s tubes were trained to port and Bromley altered course to bring *Haguro* right ahead, having decided to fire on opposite courses. At 13 minutes past, *Verulam* began to turn to starboard to fire, with *Haguro* now closing 'alarmingly fast'. Torpedoes were fired at 1.14, range on firing just below 2,000 yards. *Haguro* was also engaged by gunfire during the turn, *Verulam* getting off a few salvoes before completing her firing turn and retiring at 30 knots. Some 90 seconds after firing, Bromley saw three explosions and claimed three hits. (Subsequently those three hits were shared between *Verulam* and *Saumarez*.) *Verulam* then reduced speed and steered out to the north-east to cut off the Japanese destroyer if she tried to break for Penang. All *Verulam*'s AIC crew had come rushing up on deck to see the fun and when he had collected himself after the attack and saw them, Bromley drove them all down below again to get on with their job and *Verulam* had a 'short but troublesome time sorting out who was who on the radar screen'. The position was very confused but, significantly, by 1.20 Bromley reported that there were only five echoes on *Verulam*'s screens—four of the flotilla and the wreck of *Haguro*.

In *Haguro*, Motora was searching the sea on the port side through binoculars when he heard the look-out shouting 'Torpedo tracks!' *Haguro* was actually turning to starboard at full speed when the torpedoes hit her port side, abreast of the three forward 8-inch gun turrets. Motora saw all three turrets burst into flame from internal fires, as the ship listed quickly over to 30° to port and stayed there. Speed fell off rapidly to 16–18 knots. All electric power had failed and all guns went silent. After a short time the two after 8-inch turrets and some of the AA guns began firing again (possibly, thought Motora, operating in manual control) but their fire was scattered, uncoordinated and, according to Motora, ineffective.

In the heat of the moment, everybody on *Haguro*'s bridge had quite forgotten *Kamikaze* who was trailing only 300 metres astern. *Haguro*'s sudden turns and reduction in speed caused *Kamikaze* almost to collide with her. *Kamikaze* shot past *Haguro* and then began to circle her. The men on *Haguro*'s bridge were only reminded of *Kamikaze* when they saw her abeam of them, and Admiral Hashimoto ordered her to Penang, in Motora's words, 'without concerning to *Haguro*'.

In the meantime Sugiura ordered smoke but as *Haguro* was by now almost stopped the smoke rose vertically and ineffectually into the air. After another torpedo hit, the engine-room 'went silent', and the ship stopped. *Haguro* was now under fire from both sides. Everyone on her bridge crouched low behind the bridge plating under a hail of splinters and close range shells. One 4·7-inch scored a direct hit on *Haguro*'s bridge, killing Admiral Hashimoto and most of the bridge officers and crew instantaneously. Motora and another officer, a paymaster, survived, miraculously unharmed. Captain Sugiura also survived but was very badly wounded in the stomach. For a while Motora lay unconscious under the wreckage of the bridge until the impact of another torpedo hit brought him to his senses. *Haguro* was stopped, listing further to port, with some of her close-range weapons still in action, but only sporadically, as individual crews were able to load and fire them.

Captain Power never saw *Kamikaze* again after she passed down his port side but he did see and hear a 'biggish explosion' over on his port beam. Over in *Venus*, Midshipman Robathan saw 'a huge mushroom of red flame billowing up into black smoke, followed by a dying down to a red glow, which remained and pinpointed the enemy cruiser until she sank. We thought it was *Saumarez* who simultaneously reported that she was hit, but our fears were soon allayed when we were told that it was the cruiser and fire, especially 8-inch, ceased to come from her'.

Virago and *Vigilant* also saw the explosion and thought it was *Saumarez*. Power himself 'did not give it much thought at the time, rather assuming that it must be one of the flotilla in trouble, as I had lost track of the enemy destroyer. The rest of the flotilla saw it and apparently eagerly assumed that this marked the end of yet another Dictator. Such was happily not the case'. The explosion was almost certainly two torpedoes colliding and mutually detonating.

Everywhere *Haguro* turned there seemed to be another destroyer waiting for her. The torpedo hits reported by Motora were very probably those fired by *Venus* and *Virago*, who were next to attack. *Venus* had missed her first chance due to a number of factors: the Sub-Lieutenant had stayed too long down in the AIC, where he was apparently the only officer available to sum up the chances of a torpedo attack and inform de Chair. The lighting in the AIC was too bright, so that the Sub was night-blind for some time after reaching the bridge (in contrast to *Saumarez*, where Power insisted on minimum lighting and himself had gone up to the bridge and easily accustomed himself to the dark without the aid of red goggles). Finally, when *Venus* missed her bow shot, de Chair was preoccupied with trying to turn the ship to bring the sights on rather than changing the angling of the torpedoes.

Venus now, however, made up for previous errors and omissions. Having turned away to the north-west, *Venus* started to gain bearing on *Haguro* who was soon abeam. *Venus* opened fire with main armament and soon began hitting with all four guns at a range of just over 6,000 yards. They could see that *Haguro* was on fire aft. *Venus* reduced speed and soon came under some inaccurate fire from *Haguro*. By radar, *Venus*' gunnery seemed very effective. The Chief Gunner's Mate later told de Chair that sitting in the Transmitting Station he could 'see' *Venus*' salvoes hitting and also the enemy's shells apparently hitting *Venus*, causing him to duck involuntarily in his seat every time. *Venus* was surrounded by shell splashes but was fortunately not hit.

After a few salvoes, 'A' gun in *Venus* suffered a misfire. The gun's captain Able Seaman J. Greenhalgh ordered the mounting cleared of ready-use ammunition and told the rest of the gun's crew to stand back whilst he opened the breech and assisted by AB A. M. Dawson withdrew the misfired cartridge. The gun was in action again after three minutes, instead of the thirty minutes laid down in the gunnery manual. 'B' gun, firing starshell, jammed on the 12th round leaving Leading Seaman Marshall, the captain of the gun, disconsolately watching 'A', 'X' and 'Y', in Robathan's words, 'to do all the bashing with SAP later on. Then followed some very pretty shooting with 'A' gun from 6,000 yards to 2,000 yards and getting a deuce of a lot of hits. Towards the end when the cruiser was stopped and we just blazed away from about 1,500 yards and hitting every time. It was good to watch the shell go surely on its way and one could say whether it was going to hit or not before it got there. We fired 40 odd SAP and we reckon on 60% hits *at least*.'

Robathan had been officer of the quarters at 'B' gun and, when it jammed, he realized the whole action was likely to be over in a few minutes and went up on the bridge. De Chair was delighted to see him, having been hard-pressed to pass orders to the voice-pipe through his steward. An extra officer on the bridge was invaluable and de Chair stationed Robathan by the voice-pipe to pass com-

15 Ordinary Seaman Norman Poole, the radar watchkeeper in *Venus*, who insisted 'to the point of insubordination' that he had a ship in radar contact, and so led to the action against *Haguro*.

16 Torpedo party on board *Venus* at Trincomalee.

17 Captain Power visiting the Japanese heavy cruiser *Myoko*, sister ship to *Haguro* in Johore Strait after the war. Lofty Power, unamused by grinning Japanese remark. In the background, left and partly obscured, Lieutenant P. Moss RNVR; right Lieutenant Tony Tyers.

mand orders and to keep an ear cocked for TBS messages (of which there were 365 in one hour).

For his second attack de Chair ordered torpedo depth settings of 10 to 14 feet, in accordance with the torpedo manual settings for a ship of *Haguro*'s size and draught. Privately de Chair had thought the nine-foot settings previously ordered endangered the flotilla themselves, a point well taken by *Venus*' engine-room staff.

At the height of the action, *Venus*' Engineer Officer, Lieutenant (E) J. W. Galen heard a mysterious 'whirring' noise above the sound of the main engines. He asked the engine-room artificer at the starboard main engine throttle, 'What do you make of that noise?'

'Sounds like a torpedo going up the ship's side, sir!'

A few seconds later Galen heard a second similar 'whirring' noise. When he offered a cigarette to Chief Engine Room Artificer S. J. Perrett, his hands were shaking so much he could hardly hold the packet. He apologized for his nerves, but the Chief said 'That's not nerves, sir, that's just excitement!'

Venus went in for her second attack at 1.24 and fired a salvo of six torpedoes in local control, range 2,500 yards. At 1.30 de Chair put the helm over to turn away under cover of smoke after he thought he heard the report 'All tubes fired'. In fact, in the noise and confusion of the action, de Chair had misheard. The report had been '*After* tubes fired' and there were two torpedoes left in the forward tubes. When he was told this, 'thinking of Tovey at Jutland', de Chair headed back towards *Haguro* again at 1.39 but had to break off his attack when *Vigilant* signalled, 'Keep clear; am attacking with torpedoes'.

Meanwhile, *Virago* had been somewhat 'left out in the cold' because she initially shadowed the enemy from a range of 10–12 miles, lost contact and had to turn in to close and relocate the enemy. White actually sighted *Haguro* from *Virago*'s bridge as early as 1.03 am, but as *Virago* closed she was hampered in her approach by *Venus*, crowding in from the port side, and every time she tried to begin another attack her firing range, as White said, 'was fouled by one friendly ship or another'. White twice had to change his angle of attack as he approached, so that his torpedo crews had to train the tubes to and fro, struggling to keep their balance on the deck as the ship heeled first this way and then that. *Haguro*'s fire had been reduced to single 5-inch shots, in local control, with occasional sporadic ripples of close range fire. At 2,500 yards range *Virago* fired a rocket flare which burst above and behind the enemy, showing *Haguro* almost stopped with a huge list of some 40° to port. In spite of her adventures, *Virago*'s torpedo attack was very well co-ordinated with *Venus*, as it turned out, her salvo going away at 1.27, two minutes after *Venus*. Only seven of *Virago*'s torpedoes were fired because the ship was swinging a little too fast and the torpedo sights came off the target before the eighth torpedo could be launched. But *Virago* was credited with two hits, and *Venus* one. Meanwhile, *Virago*'s main armament had opened fire, having been given a splendid aiming point by a rash gunner in *Haguro* who had fired tracer on the rocket flare. *Haguro* could be seen almost completely enveloped in smoke astern as *Virago* heeled away.

The 5-inch shell-hit amidships had thrown *Saumarez* into a temporary state of confusion. Communications between bridge and steering, and bridge and engine-room, had been cut. The great cloud of smoke and steam prevented those on the bridge from seeing aft and those aft from seeing forward. On the bridge, they thought that the after part of the ship had been destroyed, or at best, very badly damaged. Aft, everybody thought that the bridge had been hit and all on it had been killed.

Amidships, the Captain's Secretary determined to take remedial action. 'Between us (and the bridge) was a volcano of flames and steam, and the noise was paralysing. Only one thing was clear in my mind—that the bridge had been blown away, and that I must get to my emergency station, the emergency steering position just abaft the hole where the funnel had been. So, taking my Petty Officer Writer, Raymond Pollitt, from the gun's crew, I went forward along the catwalk. We both knew the drill by heart and within seconds we had disconnected the bridge steering and taken over the conning of the ship from our emergency steering position. The little wooden wheel came alive in my hands, and I turned and faced aft, my back to the intense heat coming from the wreckage of the funnel. I put the helm hard-a-port, more to see whether she would answer the helm than for any other reason; but Pollitt was shouting in my ear "Ram her! Ram her!". Then a figure appeared through the steam and darkness from forward and screamed "Put it back—revert to main steering". So we did, at once.'

In fact, the damage to *Saumarez* was, as Power said, 'ridiculously small'. The exaggerated list to starboard was caused by the wheel hard-a-port, the thrust of the starboard screw and the ship's own light state, being short of fuel; after remaining longer than expected, for some reason, the list disappeared and marvellously, *Saumarez* came upright again. It was thought that the gyro compass had 'toppled' due to the shock of the shell hits and Captain Power summoned Knollys on the bridge to ship the magnetic compass. Knollys could see the gyro compass repeater swinging rapidly but he discovered this was because *Saumarez* still had hard port wheel on. The gyro was in fact merely recording the actual situation; as Knollys said, 'The ship was about to turn round in a sharp circle, with the enemy about twelve hundred yards away.' As the steam which had filled the Low Power Electrical Machinery Compartment subsided, machines were restarted, fuses replaced, circuits reconnected. Lights came on again and life began to return to normal. Men dried out their telephone receivers, emptied water from their shoes, and realized that they were still alive and, with a little luck, might even go on living. The only damage to the ship's fighting efficiency were some aerials which had been shot away, and the loss of No 1 Boiler Room.

Down below 'Spud' Yates was still in the fan flat above the boiler-room. 'I went back to the boiler-room air lock and the ship's doctor, Lieutenant "Mick" Evans, asked me how many men were trapped below and I told him. He gallantly tried to get down

137

to them but was hit by the tremendous heat. He realized that there was little chance of anybody down there surviving. I was then hustled along to the sick bay by the sick berth attendant and treated for scalds. Marten was already in a cot when I got there.' Marten and Yates were taken to hospital in Trincomalee, where Marten died of his injuries. Yates' own ordeal by scalding kept him in hospital for some weeks, after which he rejoined *Saumarez* in Durban, and was later awarded a very well-won Conspicuous Gallantry Medal.

Saumarez had been steaming in 'units', an arrangement of main machinery designed specifically to minimise precisely this kind of action damage. In action, the steam supply from No 1 Boiler Room supplied only the port main turbine and hence drove the port propeller shaft, being totally isolated from the steam supply from No 2 Boiler Room which likewise drove the starboard main turbine and the starboard propeller shaft. The two supplies could, however, be cross-connected at will. 'Spud' Yates' opposite number in No 2 Boiler Room shut an isolating valve on the steam pipes from the No 1 Boiler Room, while the engine-room staff cross-connected the supply from No 2 Boiler Room to both main turbines. The ship could now proceed on both shafts, albeit at a reduced speed.

Meanwhile, Commander (E) Geoffrey Robins and Stoker Petty Officer Enoch Davies, of the damage control party, tackled the situation in the boiler-room. They found the shell still lodged in the boiler. Fortunately for *Saumarez*, the shell had only partially exploded. Its body was still intact and only the nose portion had sheared off. The damage done was astonishingly slight. A full detonation there might have broken the ship's back. Telling the damage control parties to clear the area, Robins, with Davies' help, manhandled the shell from inside the boiler, carried it up to the upper deck and threw it over the side. Later, the bodies of Elliott and Hendren were recovered. Amongst those present at this very melancholy task was Leading Stoker A. M. Watson, a particular chum of Elliott's. He had donned a smoke mask and tried to enter the boiler-room with Commander Robins and PO Davies but had been driven back by the heat. It was in fact nearly half an hour before the boiler room had cooled enough for Robins to be able to lead the way below.

Robins evidently had a somewhat diabolical sense of humour. He now rang the bridge to report an unexploded shell in the boiler, waited until his sensational news had caused the maximum *furore* of consternation on the bridge and Power had even ordered 'Hands to emergency stations', and then added: 'But it's all right, not to worry, we've thrown it over the side'. Robins' sense of humour was evidently shared by some of his department. According to Knollys, a stoker emerged on deck at the height of the action and enquired what was up? On being told it was a Japanese cruiser, he said 'Blimey I thought it was a junk!' and promptly dived below again. Robins received a DSC, Enoch Davies a DSM, both very well merited.

On the bridge, Captain Power had more than his Engineer Officer's sense of humour to occupy him. He had inadvertently left the telegraphs to 'Full' and *Saumarez* had retired some five miles to the north-west. Power had meant to allow time for the ship to collect herself and feel herself all over for injuries but not to remove himself so far from the scene. The loss of his aerials meant he now had to relay his orders through *Verulam*. At 1.40 he reported 'Cruiser sinking' to the C-in-C. At the same time, he knew the cruiser was almost gone, and he knew that *Vigilant* still had her full outfit of eight torpedoes left. He wanted the others to withdraw, to leave the field clear for *Vigilant* but, as he said, there was now 'an apparent and possibly excusable mutiny in the flotilla'. The rest of the flotilla 'were snarling round the carcass like a lot of starving wolves round a dying bull. I was too far away to make out what was going on and told them all except *Vigilant* (who I knew had torpedoes) to come away and join me, with a view to getting formed up and the situation in hand. Of course they did nothing of the sort. I should not have done myself'. At the same time, Power could not close the scene himself because the rest of the flotilla were 'intent on firing torpedoes in unknown directions to finish off the enemy'.

Vigilant had had to make a long board out to the east to get into her sector and like *Virago*, she had been rather crowded out by other ships. Furthermore, she had been plagued all night with defects in her 293 radar presentation and in the main ARL plotting table. The radar screen was difficult to focus, so that echoes were not presented sharply enough defined to plot properly, and every time the ship heeled or altered course all the echoes disappeared. Thus for much of the time Argles was only able to get an incomplete picture of events as they unfolded. At 1 am the radar set failed altogether and it was nearly a quarter of an hour before frantic work by the radar mechanics brought some response. This gap covered the crucial time of *Saumarez'* attack and when *Vigilant*'s radar was working again it at once showed a ship contact dead ahead. A rocket flare was fired which illuminated a ship shrouded in smoke or steam or both, obviously badly damaged and very probably enemy. Jubilantly Argles signalled, 'Am illuminating the enemy'. Captain Power, suddenly bathed in brilliant light from *Vigilant*'s flare, and seeing *Vigilant* herself clearly advancing in a belligerent manner, replied dampingly, 'Think that is me'.

At 1.30 *Vigilant* signalled *Saumarez* to ask if there was a target left and at 1.36 was told to close and sink the cruiser. *Vigilant* was at this time to the north of *Haguro* and when a starshell jammed in 'B' turret (one of several starshell mishaps in the flotilla that night) *Vigilant* asked *Virago* to illuminate the target. Guided by *Virago*'s flares, *Vigilant* steered south and then turned east at 1.50 to fire a full salvo of torpedoes one minute later at a now almost stationary *Haguro*, range about 1,800 yards. The cruiser was lying deep in the water like a sodden log, with her upper deck awash almost from end to end.

To Argles' surprise and chagrin there was no obvious sign of a hit from any of *Vigilant*'s torpedoes, although one of the Bofors crews reported an explosion which might have been a hit. *Vigilant*

140

was credited with one probable hit, but Argles himself concluded that all theirs had missed. It was all the more surprising and galling because *Vigilant*'s Torpedo Firing Officer had a reputation as something of a 'Dead Eye Dick'. He, in fact, had hit the submarine chaser with one torpedo, although she had been jinking about like a snipe at the time, during the attack on the Japanese convoy on 26 March. *Vigilant* had used a binocular attachment on the bridge torpedo sight, which was known to have a degree of backlash in the fitting. Although the deflection chosen was thought to cover this defect fully, Argles ruefully concluded that it had not been enough. It was not the torpedoes' fault. They were all seen to enter the water and run on course correctly.

However, as she turned away after firing torpedoes, *Vigilant* opened fire with all four 4·7-inch guns and soon began to register some 60% hits under *Haguro*'s bridge and forward turrets, one of which caused a large internal explosion amidships. *Vigilant*'s midships Bofors also opened fire, spraying the forward superstructure with shells. *Vigilant* was answered by one solitary round, probably an individual 5-inch, from *Haguro*.

Virago now suggested switching on fighting lights. Power could have kicked himself for not thinking of it before. All his previous experience—at Matapan, Normandy and off the Norwegian coast—had shown the absolute necessity of burning fighting lights in a close confused situation. Fighting lights were shining at the flotilla's yard-arms and the scene therefore was a little clearer when at 1.51 Power ordered *Venus* to 'close and make a job of it'. The flotilla had already fired 37 torpedoes—*Saumarez*, *Verulam* and *Vigilant*, 8 each, *Virago* 7 and *Venus* 6—but this cruiser was clearly, as Captain Power said, 'a very hardy specimen—still afloat after six hits'.

Venus had already signalled at 1.47 that she was attacking again with her two remaining torpedoes. At 2.02 am *Venus* closed to 1,200 yards, when *Haguro* was dead in the water, and fired her two remaining torpedoes. From the bridge Robathan saw the

141

detonations. 'There was a lot of starshell in the air and it blended very well with the vivid prolonged forked lightning which went on incessantly. Although the scene was set under lowering clouds it did not rain and the visibility was good and clear. When we closed in, firing the whole time, we opened up with Bofors and their pink tracers were very spectacular as they curved towards the now stopped cruiser with its deck awash and after part covered with billowing thick black smoke. Then at last, in the light of some dozen starshell, we fired our last two fish in local control and there was a tense minute, which dragged on for hours, before one after the other, two huge grey shapes leapt into the air, looking for all the world like poplars, one hit on the stern and one on the bow.'

The news that the Japanese cruiser was going down spread in the destroyers. The bridge wings, upper decks and superstructure vantage points filled with men, all looking out over the water at *Haguro*'s last moments. Amongst the spectators was Norman Poole, who had rushed out on deck with the rest of *Venus*' AIC crew when somebody said 'She's going down'. All this sound and fury, this death and destruction, had grown from a tiny bright spot of light. *Venus* closed to 'within 500 yards, having ensured two more hits, and watched the Japanese cruiser sink, at the same time lowering the asdic dome which gave the operator the satisfaction of hearing her break up under water'. At 0206 *Venus* signalled that the cruiser had sunk. *Haguro* had gone, in position 5° 0′N 99°30′E, some 45 miles south-west of Penang.

The man least moved was Power himself. 'What did I think when she sank? The answer is not much. I knew by then she was for it and was concerned to find out how fit my own ship was, where was the enemy destroyer and was she worth searching for, and about getting back to join the fleet before running out of fuel.'

Fifty miles away *Cumberland* and *Richelieu* had seen tantalizing glimpses of starshell over the horizon at 1.15, but were too late to take part, at which as Robathan remarked, 'There was great gnashing of teeth!' In fact, in *Cumberland*, who had just missed the

Battle of the River Plate in 1939, there later appeared a sardonic little ode:

> Too late
> For the Plate
> Too slow
> For *Haguro*.

Saumarez transmitted Vs for Victory and Power signalled to the flotilla: 'Pick up survivors. Stay no more than ten minutes.' In the end, they did not stay even ten minutes and although only a 'few specimens' of survivors were required, none were picked up. 'She sank quickly,' Robathan wrote, 'and when we steamed through the bubbles we could see hardly anything, no survivors, perhaps a boat and just one winking light like a calcium flare. Miraculously "Lanchester" carbines appeared on "B" gun-deck all ready to discourage any saboteurs among the survivors. We had both our 20-inch searchlights on and we felt most insecure. But *Vigilant* saw an aircraft with lights switched on circling us (or so she said) and we got to hell out of it.'

Amongst those in the water were Motora and Captain Sugiura. Motora saw his Captain floating with other survivors but he 'died soon'.

The aircraft was almost certainly imaginary (as even *Vigilant* later admitted) but the flotilla were well within the range of enemy airfields and Power 'was not taking chances and took the whole party away at once'.

At 1.54, during the most hectic part of the action, *Venus'* HF direction-finder operator picked up a Japanese surface unit transmitting on a bearing of 105°, with a ground wave transmission giving a range of less than 15 miles away. The message consisted of 36 words of 4-sign code and was transmitted to Singapore, bearing the highest degree of priority. It was repeated at 2.07 but at neither time was Singapore heard to give a receipt. Allied Intelligence, however, picked up fragments of a message from an unknown operator, time of origin some three hours after *Haguro*'s sinking. The signal described an action fought by *Haguro* and *Kamikaze* against an Allied force of two (possibly cruisers) and a destroyer in position 04°49′N 99°42′E. The message did not mention that *Haguro* had been sunk, but stated that one of the Japanese ships had received hits in three places, with 32 casualties, and that one of *Haguro*'s guns had been destroyed. The message also claimed the sinking of one Allied destroyer. This, in its way, was a fairly accurate resumé of the action up to the time when *Kamikaze* left the scene. The message was clearly transmitted from her, giving her version of the action.

At 2.12 am Captain Power signalled to the others, 'Out lights. Join me at full speed.' So ended what he later called 'a very satisfying and enjoyable party E & OE'. 'I remember saying during the afternoon,' wrote Midshipman Robathan, 'what an awful joke it would be if we sunk her on our own, without the big ships, aircraft and submarines!'

[6]

AFTERMATH

AT 2.40 AM ON 16 MAY Captain Power signalled his official report of the sinking of *Haguro* to the Commander-in-Chief. Repeated to Admiral Walker and Patterson, the signal was routed 'Immediate' and classified 'Confidential'. 'Enemy cruiser sunk. Enemy destroyer unaccounted for. *Saumarez* one boiler-room out of action. Remainder of 26th DF NOT repeat NOT damaged. My position course and speed 005°00′N 099°35′E–295–25 knots.' Twenty-five knots was full power on *Saumarez*' remaining boiler, with its steam supply now cross-connected to supply both main turbines.

On the bridges and in the AICs of the destroyers men were so keyed up by the tension of the action that they could not relax. It was some time before the excitement died down. All those present knew that they had just passed through one of the most climactic experiences of their whole lives. They would remember the last couple of hours, in ever increasing detail, until their dying days. Already men were going back over the moments of combat, remembering, adjusting, comparing, justifying, excusing, boasting, preparing their own memories of the action. Already, a received version of events was beginning to appear from the fog of war. Every man had a different memory, but as time went by they would all emerge with the same memories.

As the flotilla steamed north-west to rejoin the 5th Cruiser Squadron, the night was still not free of alarms. Two 'cloud' echoes were detected but Captain Power decided not to investigate, because the flotilla was short of fuel, and at 8 am a possible target was sighted. *Vigilant* investigated and found that it was just a small fishing vessel.

The flotilla rejoined *Richelieu* and *Cumberland* to cheers and a 'rapturous chorus of signalled bouquets and bunches of flowers', just before 10 am. At 10.55 all ships slowed down and lowered ensigns to half-mast while the bodies of Elliott and Hendren were committed to the deep.

Air activity of one kind or another had begun early and went on all day. *Emperor* flew off four Hellcats, each armed with eight 60-lb rockets, at 7 am to look for *Kurishoyo* Maru and her escort in an area between Penang and Phuket Island. They did not find them and in fact both ships reached Penang safely. The submarine chaser was slightly damaged by a mine on 18 May when on passage to Singapore, but both ships again reached harbour. As the four Hellcats returned to the fleet they were apprehended by a CAP, having failed to switch on their IFF, but were happily identified in time, and were escorted back to the carriers, passing over the returning 26th Destroyer Flotilla some 40 miles from Force 61. Meanwhile six Hellcats from *Khedive* set off to strafe the airfield of Lhokseumawe, in northern Sumatra. Two turned back with radio failures but the others went on, set fire to one Tojo fighter on the airfield and shot up a locomotive on a track nearby, leaving it on fire and blowing off satisfactory clouds of steam.

Nubian had been searching for Burns' dinghy since 10 pm the previous evening and at dawn 851 Squadron flew off two Avengers to join her. The day was cloudy, with broken cloud up to 20,000 feet and a cloud ceiling of only 1,000 feet for much of the way. Visibility was only about 15 miles and, once again, the searching aircraft actually flew over the dinghy, at about 700 feet, without sighting it. When they reached *Nubian*, the Avengers separated, one flying north the other flying south, but though they both searched for some hours, covering an area of some 60 square miles, neither sighted anything and had to return to the carrier. Various aircraft had passed close overhead on four occasions, without

146

sighting the dinghy. Never was the fatal lack of some means of signalling more clearly demonstrated.

From about 8 am onwards there was an almost continuous succession of 'bogeys' on Force 63's radar screens. The Japanese Army and Navy had resolved their disagreements over providing air cover and, obviously alarmed and infuriated by the loss of *Haguro*, began to mount the kind of air effort which might well have saved her the day before. At 9 am a CAP of four Seafires from *Hunter* was vectored out to the southward and after some twenty minutes sighted four Oscars 500 feet below them. Two of the Seafires gave chase and although the Oscars got away, one was at least damaged, flying off with 'one oleo leg down'.

The 26th Destroyer Flotilla rejoined just after noon, during another 'Aircraft Warning Red', with *Nigeria* and *Queen Elizabeth* putting up an intense AA barrage. However the bogeys, another group of four Oscars, did not come close to the fleet.

Fuller simply could not accept that Burns and his crew were either dead or prisoners of the Japanese. When the first two searching Avengers returned, he asked for all available Avengers to mount a full scale search. This was refused but Sub-Lieutenant Fletcher, a particular friend of Burns, asked and was given permission to fly another search sortie. Fletcher flew off at 10.30 and carried out a box search to within sight of Phuket Island but again without sighting anything. He stayed as long as he could and after some difficulty in finding the fleet (who had had to alter course to avoid another air attack) he eventually landed on just after 6 pm that evening, with tanks very nearly empty.

More air attacks had begun in the afternoon. Two Oscars dived on the fleet from about 7,000 feet just after 4 pm. They penetrated the AA barrage but when pursued by Seafires from the CAP they jettisoned their bombs and escaped low over the sea towards Sumatra. At 5.25 pm four Hellcats from *Emperor*, led by the acting CO of 800 Squadron, Lieutenant H. de Witt R. Neth.N., came out of cloud and surprised two Mitsubishi A6M3 'Hamps' which, however, recovered quickly and vanished back into the cloud.

This was all much more Japanese air effort than the fleet had ever experienced before, and it was by no means finished for the day. Another 'bogey' was soon picked up, range 64 miles, to the south of the fleet. Hellcats and Seafires were vectored out to engage them. The Hellcats caught a glimpse of the enemy through a gap in cloud but the intruders escaped.

It was thought that the 26th Destroyer Flotilla would have only 10% fuel remaining after their exertions. But even that was an overestimate, especially for *Virago*, who had only 18 tons of fuel left and during the afternoon reported her boiler-room oil fuel pumps were losing suction. Her oil fuel filters were clogged, because of the low level of the fuel, and the debris shaken up and drawn into them during the high speed and violent manœuvring of the night before. So, when the last CAP had been landed on, *Virago* was ordered to close *Hunter* from astern and refuel.

The last air attacks began as darkness was falling. *Virago* had approached to within three cables of the carrier's stern when another Oscar was sighted by the midships Bofors crew in *Saumarez*. The Bofors opened fire and alerted the rest of the fleet as the Oscar flew towards *Virago*, clearly aiming to attack *Hunter*, ahead of her. The combined gunfire of the fleet, especially of *Virago*, who was nearest, seemed to deter the Japanese pilot. He dropped his single bomb from about 5,000 feet, peeled off to the east and made his escape.

As this air attack developed, *Virago* was ordered to let go the fuelling hose and drop back half a cable astern of *Hunter*. As *Virago* did so, White could see from his bridge the bomb falling towards *Virago*'s stern. He ordered the helm hard-a-port and the stern began to swing. But before the ship could respond fully the bomb hit the water about 30 yards off *Virago*'s port quarter. The bomb was of the fragmentation type, designed to cause the maximum amount of damage to ships' superstructures and injuries to personnel. *Virago*'s after damage control station was a small compartment, not much more than a cupboard, in the after superstructure, and most of the damage control and first aid parties were standing in the flat beside or on deck in the open. The hail of steel splinters from the bomb cut through those men, killing four outright and wounding eight more. More splinters pierced the ship's side and smashed furniture and fittings in the after seamen's mess-deck but there was no underwater damage to the hull and the survivors of the damage control party soon had matters in hand. *Virago*'s Engineer Officer, Lieutenant-Commander (E) C. W. Baker, took charge of the situation admirably, supervising the clearing of damage and ensuring that fuelling continued, until *Virago* had taken in some 110 tons of fuel. *Venus* also fuelled and then passed her doctor and sick berth attendant over to *Virago* at 10.30 that night, *Virago*'s own sick berth attendant being one of the casualties.

The next day, 17 May, *Royalist, Nigeria, Khedive, Shah* and the 11th Destroyer Flotilla were detached to return to Trincomalee while the remainder steamed to a patrol position some 300 miles south-west of the Six Degree Channel for more fighter and anti-shipping sweeps. But nothing was sighted. It was high time the 26th Destroyer Flotilla was also detached. During the night of 18th/19th the weather worsened and *Virago* asked if the force could steer more to the southward as the motion of the sea was causing her wounded some discomfort. A little after 9 am the next morning Captain Power's ships were at last free to return to Ceylon, just as the fleet were investigating another 'bogey' to the northeast (which proved to be a RAF Catalina not using IFF).

The 26th Destroyer Flotilla entered Trincomalee harbour at 6.30 on the morning of 21 May. Despite the early hour, the decks of every ship in harbour were lined with men, ready to cheer the flotilla to their berths. *Virago* and *Saumarez* went directly alongside the destroyer depot ship *Woolwich* to repair action damage. While doing so, the flotilla's doings changed from high drama to low comedy. *Virago* had difficulty in coming alongside and *Venus*, following immediately behind her, suffered a loss of electrical power supply to the steering motor. De Chair had the mortification of having to hoist two black balls—the signal for 'ship not under command'—under the eyes of the whole cheering fleet, until power was repaired and the steering restored.

Admiral Sir Arthur John Power, who had returned to Ceylon on 19th, went on board each of the destroyers that forenoon and spoke to the assembled ship's companies. That evening the flotilla's officers had a celebration party in *Woolwich*'s wardroom. Songs were sung, speeches were made, drinks were consumed, Lofty Power was ceremonially presented with a small model of a *Nachi* class heavy cruiser.

A few weeks later the honours and awards were announced, and there were a great number of medals to be 'wetted'. Besides those already mentioned in the narrative, there were Bars to their DSCs for de Chair and Meryon, and DSCs all round for Bromley, Argles and White, for Stobie and Parkinson in *Saumarez* and for Paxton in *Venus*. There were DSMs for Petty Officer Writer Raymond Pollitt, Petty Officer L. Finch, and Stoker Petty Officer H. Cracknell, all of *Saumarez*, and for Petty Officer Albert Kisby and Stoker Petty Officer Ernest Paul of *Venus*. A long list of officers and men, in the carriers and in the destroyers, were mentioned in dispatches.

With Commander Robins' DSC, 'Spud' Yates' CGM, DSMs for Paul, Cracknell and Enoch Davies, and several mentions in dispatches and in congratulatory signals, the flotilla's engine-room departments received the recognition that they had richly earned. The 26th Destroyer Flotilla had steamed for 330 miles at 27 knots in the search for *Haguro* and no ship's main machinery had faltered. The sensations of all those down below, unable to see what was happening but having to rely on sounds, messages and rumours, was described by Stoker Petty Officer Harry Cater in *Verulam*. 'Some time after 11 pm I heard the pipe "We hope to engage the enemy in an hour's time". That cheered me up and also the remark made by the Petty Officer I relieved on watch at midnight. "Best of luck, you'll need it"—he was a Scot, not dour

but sour! When the action did come it was all "Half speed . . .
Full . . . Stop . . . Prepare to tow . . ." (that was when *Saumarez*
got hit in the boiler-room). Someone rang from the engine-room
"Harry, it's like bonfire night! Her ammo's going up!" We did
have the luck with us but it was very hard on the nerves and I
nearly bit my pipe stem in half. Ruined several pipes that way in
other actions.'

For Captain Power himself there was a Bar to his DSO, an
award which, in the circumstances, could not be described as
over-generous. It was common gossip, though it was only gossip,
in the flotilla and in the fleet at the time that the Commander-in-
Chief had recommended Manley Power for a Victoria Cross. The
general opinion then was that if Lofty had sunk that cruiser off
Norway in May, 1940, instead of off Penang in May, 1945, a few
days after VE Day, he certainly would have got his VC.

Power himself was aware that the sinking of *Haguro* was an
action which never got the notice it deserved, and 'was conscious
that this to a large degree was my own fault because I had avoided
the press from dislike of that medium and from a strong dislike
for personal publicity. Looking back, this was a mistake on my part
because it deprived the flotilla of well-deserved publicity, which
was not my aim.'

Not everybody in *Saumarez* had cause to congratulate himself.
One Able Seaman had deserted his post in the presence of the
enemy—which, according to very ancient naval tradition and also
by actual legal definition of the Naval Discipline Act, was a
capital offence. The charge read 'For that he, Able Seaman of
His Majesty's Ship SAUMAREZ, then being a person subject to
the Naval Discipline Act, did, when acting as starboard forward
lookout at 0116 on the 16th day of May, 1945, in the presence of
the enemy, desert his post.'

There was one witness for the prosecution, Lieutenant
Learmond, the Torpedo Control Officer, who testified that the
accused's action station was on the bridge, that the ship was at the
time closely engaged with the enemy, that noticing the accused's

absence from his post he assumed him to have been blown over the side by enemy salvoes, only to discover him, after the action, hiding behind the director tower at the after end of the bridge. The accused was found guilty, sentenced to six months' imprisonment and dismissed the Service. Some of Captain Power's own staff thought he might have been more lenient. 'I am, I must say,' wrote Reay Parkinson, 'surprised that this episode has been perpetuated [i.e. in accounts of the action]. Nothing could persuade Lofty not to pursue this unfortunate man, but Lofty did.'

The episode showed the other side of the human face in the presence of great danger although Power himself, like Parkinson, was surprised that the incident is still remembered and mentioned. 'The plain fact is that he had, and admitted he had, deserted his post in action. By my standards and training there was no alternative. There was a long delay after initial remand because we were on passage to South Africa. In that interval I made sure that he would have the best possible defence, with Surgeon Lieutenant Evans as prisoner's friend. Evans found him to be mentally retarded and got psychiatric support from Simonstown Hospital. I myself, as prosecutor, testified to his good conduct, willingness and excellence as a lookout. Had I dealt with this case summarily, much earlier as it would have been, this business of mental retardation and diminished responsibility would never have emerged and he would have been little better off. I was myself surprised that the Court Martial paid so little heed to the plea of diminished responsibility, which was well presented in Court. In fact I had always rather liked this little man and felt sorry for him. In discussing afterwards with Evans he told me that the sentence meant little to the victim, far less than if I had been personally unkind to him, and that he would feel nice and safe in prison!'

While Captain Power's ships celebrated, their victims had been picking up the survivors. Early on 16 May a Japanese signal had been intercepted by Allied Intelligence reporting that a destroyer (*Kamikaze*) and a submarine chaser, clearly *Kurishoyo* Maru's escort, No 57, had left Penang to rescue survivors. The submarine chaser later reported that she had 'reached the scene of the disaster' and sighted nothing. *Kamikaze* had more luck. According to Motora, she returned to the scene at about 4 pm that day and picked up 400 of *Haguro*'s people. By Motora's account, some 800 were lost. It must have been a bitter task for Kasuga in *Kamikaze*. The tradition of the Imperial Japanese Navy was attack, and then attack again. He had had to leave the battle scene, on the direct orders of his superior officer, the clear implication being that his ship was thought a liability in a night encounter. Possibly she had no torpedoes, almost certainly no radar, and Hashimoto obviously feared the dangers of colliding with *Kamikaze* more than he valued her contribution to the action.

Kurishoyo Maru No 2 and SC 57 had survived but not for long. On 5 June, Force 65 of *Tartar* (D.10), *Eskimo*, *Nubian*, *Penn* and *Paladin* sailed from Trincomalee for another anti-shipping 'club run' between the Nicobars and Sabang (Operation IRREGULAR). A fuelling group, Force 64, of the RFA *Olwen* escorted by *Test* sailed from Rangoon. On the 7th *Paladin* went to the Batu Islands, off the west coast of Sumatra, to evacuate a clandestine party and stayed on patrol in the area until she was relieved by *Penn*. On the 12th *Penn* sank a camouflaged Japanese Type 'A' Landing Craft, with 20 troops on board. She too was relieved by the submarine *Trident* on 15 June.

Four days earlier, *Trident* had been on patrol off Diamond Point when she sighted and reported a large Japanese landing ship with an escort, heading northwards. After the loss of *Haguro*, the Japanese had decided to carry on with evacuations using auxiliaries, sailing vessels—any craft they had—and this was *Kurishoyo* and her attendant on another mission.

Liberators of 222 Group RAF were to have begun searches at dawn, but Force 65 forestalled them. Shortly before 5.30 am on 12 June, when Force 65 was some 14 miles north-west of Rondo Island (which was 20 miles NE of Sabang), two small radar echoes were detected to the south-east. The masts of the two ships were soon sighted on the port bow and *Eskimo* and *Nubian* opened fire at 5.52. *Nubian* sank SC 57 by gunfire at 6.19 and a minute later *Kurishoyo* blew up and sank after two torpedo hits from a salvo from *Eskimo*.

Tartar's 'Y' Party reported Japanese air activity and Force 65 did not pause to pick up survivors, who were in any case reluctant to be saved. *Nubian* passed over the spot where *Kurishoyo* had sunk and men on her deck saw thirty or forty Japanese swimming in the sea close to starboard. 'They were all wearing red and white skull caps and looked like a large water polo team.' None of the team wanted to be picked up.

The expected air attacks did develop as Force 65 retired to the north-east and one bomb exploded only fifteen yards from *Nubian*'s port side but fortunately did no damage. The patrol ended on 15 June and from then on *Test* and sloops of the Royal Indian Navy maintained a patrol along the Tenasserim Coast until 27 July. Patrols were also maintained between the Andamans and the coast of Burma by the cruiser *Phoebe* (who was relieved on 1 June by *Ceylon*) HMIS *Sutlej* and *Cauvery*. From 15 June, the frigate *Lossie*, and the RIN sloops *Kodri*, *Kodabari*, *Kistna* and *Narbada* took it in turns to maintain a single-ship patrol. None of them saw any enemy activity at all.

Kamikaze went on to survive the war although, by the end, she had become in a sense the Jonah of the Japanese 10th Area Fleet. Her very presence as escort was a sure portent of disaster. She had accompanied *Haguro* on her last voyage and on 8 June she was also escorting *Haguro*'s sister ship *Ashigara*, the one remaining major warship of the 10th Area Fleet, when she carried 1,220 troops *en route* from Batavia to Singapore. *Kamikaze* had been sent on ahead when, in a brilliant attack from a difficult angle in the mined and shallow waters of the Banka Strait, off Sumatra, the submarine *Trenchant* (Commander A. R. Hezlet) hit and sank *Ashigara* with five torpedoes of a salvo of eight.

Kamikaze herself was now the major surviving warship of the 10th Area Fleet and once again she accompanied another ship on her last voyage. On 12 June, *Kamikaze* left Singapore to escort the

10,000 ton tanker *Toho* Maru, bound for Rean in Cambodia with troops, as part of the evacuation Operation CHI. *Toho* Maru was bombed and sunk by USAAF aircraft off the Malayan coast on the 15th. *Kamikaze* was slightly damaged but survived and later picked up some 200 of *Toho* Maru's survivors.

Kamikaze was handed over to the Allies after the Japanese surrender and continued in service until 7 June, 1946, when she was accompanying the anti-submarine escort *Kunashiri* on a repatriation mission. *Kunashiri* ran aground on Omae Kazi, a long rocky finger of land on the east coast of Honshu. *Kamikaze* went close inshore to *Kunashiri*'s aid but ran aground herself. She was never recovered and was eventually scrapped *in situ*.

The remaining East Indies Fleet operations up to VJ Day can be briefly described. In July the fleet's minesweeping flotillas began sweeping areas which might shortly be invaded. The minesweepers were accompanied by powerful forces of carriers, cruisers and sometimes a battleship. From 5 to 7 July, while the minesweepers were working off Car Nicobar, Hellcats from *Ameer* and *Emperor* flew strikes against airfields and the cruiser *Nigeria* carried out bombardments.

On the 24th, when the sweepers had moved to Phuket Island, a mine exploded the sweeper *Plucky*'s starboard sweep. *Squirrel*, the next in line to starboard, was slow to turn to port into swept water and struck a mine. Seven ratings were killed and the ship so badly damaged she had to be sunk.

Two days later *kamikaze* bombers attacked the fleet. They were first detected by radar in *Nelson*, Admiral Walker's flagship. *Ameer* and *Emperor* both had Hellcats airborne at the time but they were not directed and the enemy were not intercepted. They were next seen from *Nelson* disappearing into cloud at about 4,000 feet. Two Val dive-bombers then dived out of the sun and were taken under fire by *Nelson* and by *Ameer*, whose gunners shot down one Val which dropped its bomb five hundred yards off the ship's bow and followed it into the sea. The cruiser *Sussex* shot down the second, which dived on the ship but hit the water some fifty yards off the starboard side. The pilot was seen to throw up his hands and cover his face as the aircraft's impetus carried it forward, so that it bounced off the sea and stove in an eight-foot length of plating just above the ship's water-line. *Sussex* later shot down another aircraft, but that evening a *kamikaze* penetrated the screen and crashed on the minesweeper *Vestal*, killing fifteen men and setting the ship on fire, so that she too had to be sunk.

Hellcats meanwhile had been striking at airfields in the Kra Isthmus and one Hellcat of 896 Squadron failed to pull out of its strafing dive and crashed into a locomotive at Dhung Dong railway station. This was the last British aircraft lost operationally over enemy territory in the East Indies. The fleet retired to Trincomalee, this operation being the last offensive action of the East Indies Fleet in World War Two.

After the atomic bombs on Hiroshima and Nagasaki, there was a lull in the East Indies theatre. The war was over, but the Japanese had not yet surrendered. General MacArthur had ordered that no local surrenders were to be accepted until he had signed the main document of Japanese surrender on board USS *Missouri* in Tokyo Bay on 2 September. The surrender of some 70,000 Japanese personnel in Singapore and Johore was signed on board *Sussex* on 4 September.

The Japanese Navy had made it clear they would not surrender the Naval Base at Singapore to the British Army. So Captain Biggs took *Rotherham* round to the naval base on the 5th and formally took over the dockyard from the Japanese. Admiral Power, flying his flag in the cruiser *Cleopatra*, received the surrender of Penang on the 2nd. Royal Marines from the cruiser *London* were landed at Sabang the same day.

Lord Mountbatten telegraphed from the Potsdom Conference to hasten preparations for Operation ZIPPER, the landing of a large number of troops at Port Dickson and Port Swettenham, as being the ideal way of re-occupying Malaya quickly, on 9 September. He received the formal surrender of the 738,400 Japanese Forces in South-East Asia at Singapore on 12 September. His opposite number, Field-Marshal Count Terauchi, had suffered a stroke on hearing of the fall of Mandalay, but was well enough to surrender his 13th Century family sword to Lord Mountbatten at Saigon on 30 November.

Saumarez had been repaired at Durban from June to August and was one of the covering force for ZIPPER. When *Saumarez* eventually arrived at Singapore, Captain Power paid a formal visit to *Myoko*, one of *Haguro*'s sister ships, which was lying in the Johore Roads, with her stern badly damaged, and two ex-German U-boats alongside her. It was an extraordinary occasion. The Japanese laid on a guard which presented arms as Captain Power came over the side. Captain Power inspected the guard and then the whole ship. He asked the Japanese captain a few questions whilst going round. The man had very little English, 'and grunted and puffed a lot as we went up and down ladders.' Power asked him what had happened to *Kamikaze* and the Japanese pointed her out, lying some distance off. Power remarked that it was a pity she had not been sunk too.

Captain Power had no love for the Japanese. He regretted not having picked up any survivors from *Haguro*, but only because Intelligence officers would have nobody to interrogate. Otherwise, they could all stay where they were, as far as he was concerned. 'It is to be hoped,' he wrote in his report, 'that sharks or other natural causes corrected my omission before any Japanese ship came out to the rescue.'

Fuller and 851 Squadron had one happy surprise after the war ended. Burns and his crew had survived. After drifting eastwards with wind and current in their dinghy for nine days without food or water, they eventually landed on a small island, some 24 miles north of Goh Lanter, where they met some native fishermen who took them to the mainland. They were handed over to the Japanese and imprisoned in a POW camp in Thailand. They were repatriated and were on their way home when *Shah* received the most welcome signal from the Flag Officer (Air) East Indies on 5 September that Burns and his crew were about to arrive at

Madras. It was decided to attempt 'to have them returned to the fold aboard *Shah*' and on the 6th Fletcher, Griffiths and Ashplant flew to RNAS Tanbaran, while *Shah* left Trincomalee for Colombo. The squadron reception committee found Burns and Sub-Lieutenant Robinson, and Petty Officer Murley, on board *Searcher*. The whole party flew back to Katukurunda on the 8th, where Fuller was waiting to welcome the returning prodigals almost before the aircraft had stopped rolling. Burns and his men were as well as could be expected after their ordeal, and very glad to be home again. *Shah* sailed for the United Kingdom on 12 September and arrived at Gourock where the Squadron dispersed and disbanded on 7 October.

Whatever Captain Power may have told the Japanese, he in fact paid the most careful attention to *Haguro*'s fate and the manner of its accomplishment. From *Saumarez'* deck, engine-room and signal logs, from the action narrative (which Alan Parsons called 'a horrible sweaty mess which I would rather have thrown straight over the side'), from his own recollections and those of *Saumarez'* officers and members of the ship's company, Captain Power wrote his Report of Proceedings, and a supplementary Appendix which he called 'Personal Impressions'. 'By putting such first-hand impressions of paper', he wrote, 'and by critical and candid analysis while matters are still fresh in the mind much value can be obtained as much for myself as for others; and perhaps the next lucky fellow may thereby be enabled to do the right thing in the *right* way for a change.'

The deprecating, faintly self-mocking, tone is typical. Captain Power was almost embarrassingly critical of himself and his handling of the affair. The torpedo attacks had been remarkably well co-ordinated. *Saumarez* had launched torpedoes at 1.13, followed by *Verulam* only a minute later. *Venus* had made her first attack at 1.25, followed by *Virago* two minutes later. Nevertheless, Captain Power criticized a number of points: the failure to switch on fighting lights early enough; the failure to train torpedo tubes to port as soon as the Plot reported the cruiser

158

going left, which would have made an easier shot and exposed *Saumarez* much less; his failure to keep the AIC properly informed so that the Plot was starved of essential information once the bridge had visual contact with the enemy (this point was more important than it seemed: had *Saumarez* lost contact, Captain Power would have demanded that the Plot lead him back to the scene of the action); and such points as *Saumarez* and *Verulam*'s omission to report that they had completed their attacks, or that the enemy was hit, or the course of their own torpedoes. (*Saumarez'* AIC was in total darkness except for emergency lights and full of steam at the relevant time but Captain Power did not make much allowances for such trifles.)

The point about own torpedo courses was well taken by the Flotilla Torpedo Staff in their later analyses of the action. *Venus'* engine-room staff had heard running torpedoes along the ship's side and analysis showed that at about 1.20 am *Venus* had indeed been endangered by the firing zone of *Verulam*'s salvo, fired at 1.14. Likewise, *Vigilant* had been endangered at about 1.36 by *Virago*'s firing zone, fired at 1.27.

The gunnery department also analysed the action, from their point of view. Except for individual guns jamming, the drills at the guns, in the Director Control Towers, and down in the Transmitting Stations, had been satisfactory. The gunners came to some interesting conclusions about their opponents. Although *Haguro*'s gunnery officer came in for some criticism, *Haguro*'s gunnery had been generally very competent, in the circumstances. *Haguro* had been faced with four, possibly five, possibly even more, fast, highly manœuvrable, and well dispersed targets. She could have picked up *Saumarez* first by radar at about 12.30 am as *Saumarez* retired southwards ahead of her; *Saumarez* would have been at about maximum range for *Haguro*'s radar until about 12.50 when *Saumarez* turned back for her final approach. By then *Verulam*, crossing *Haguro*'s bow, and *Vigilant*, on her port bow, would also be within radar range. *Haguro* probably never detected *Venus*, or even saw her, until she suddenly appeared in an attacking position and then turned away, having apparently fired.

Haguro seems to have fired seriously only at *Saumarez* and in retrospect it seems miraculous that *Saumarez* was not much more badly damaged and left helpless within close range of the enemy (in what Captain Power's understatement called an 'awkward situation'). *Haguro* clearly had some kind of blind fire radar control of her guns and from the first she was firing accurately with her 8-inch. Her line-keeping was good: although *Saumarez* was altering course violently nearly all the salvoes were in line. She opened short, but as the range closed, *Saumarez*' officers could see *Haguro*'s salvoes pitching over and straddling, with shells regularly falling close on either side. Her spread of salvoes was not more than 200 yards and her rate of fire was about 6 to 8 rounds per minute, firing salvoes from individual turrets, after one initial ten-gun broadside. Her 5-inch fire was more erratic, though faster, but her starshell fired from the 5-inch was excellent, giving brilliant light from three greenish-white stars strung together, bursting at about 1,000 feet.

Altogether, it was lucky for *Saumarez* that the hit in the forward boiler-room did not fully detonate. This may have been due to the explosive used. The inside of the shell casing, shrapnel fragments which had a shellac coating on one side, and particles of yellow amorphous lyddite powder found in *Saumarez* next day, showed that the Japanese were filling their shells with lyddite of poor quality (the 6-inch shells at Stewart Sound in March had burst with a yellowish tinge and they too, although they badly damaged *Rapid*, were actually surprisingly innocuous, considering the number of direct hits of that calibre the Japanese gunners achieved). *Kamikaze*'s gunnery, although she did score one hit on *Saumarez*' funnel, was dismissed in a few lines: 'the destroyer seemed to have little grip on the situation, and did not open fire until she was well past *Saumarez*' port beam and going away on her port quarter'. The extraordinary range of the first radar contact, on which Norman Poole had 'insisted to the point of insubordination' was a genuine target echo, was attributed to a phenomenon known as 'anomalous propagation': weather conditions had 'bent' the radar beams so that they followed the curvature of the earth to an unusual extent.

However, when all was said and done, the flotilla *had* sunk a large, fast and formidable enemy. 'The attack,' as Captain Power wrote, 'was a success; but it was by no means a perfect and polished performance. There is much to be learned from it, and plenty of room for improvement. The errors and omissions, mostly on my part in the control, were made up for by teamwork and enthusiasm. The result left me proud of the entire command.'

In forwarding Captain Power's report to the Admiralty for the information of Their Lordships, Admiral Power added that 'Captain (D), 26 and his flotilla have provided a grand example of correct conduct in the presence of the enemy. A rapid and accurate appreciation of a situation followed by initiative, judgement, skill and courage, led to the destruction of a powerful Japanese cruiser in waters where she may well have considered herself safe. Captain D, 26th Destroyer Flotilla's report is excellent and I do not wish to make any comment. The destroyers engaged the enemy at close range and have earned the admiration of the East Indies Fleet.' Later, the Supreme Commander, Admiral Lord Mountbatten, wrote in his Report to the Combined Chiefs of Staff, 'the sinking of *Haguro* is an outstanding example of a night attack by destroyers; having myself commanded a destroyer flotilla during the first two years of the war, I was able to appreciate the magnificent performance of Captain (D) 26 and his flotilla in locating and sinking such a powerful ship of the Japanese fleet, so close to one of its own bases'.

On 17 November 1945, the five destroyers of the 26th Flotilla left Colombo for the United Kingdom, via Suez and the Mediterranean, arriving early in December when the flotilla dispersed; *Saumarez* and *Venus* going to Plymouth to refit, *Virago* to Chatham, *Verulam* and *Vigilant* to the Reserve Fleet at Harwich.

Saumarez, *Venus* and *Virago* went out to the Mediterranean to form the 3rd Destroyer Flotilla, being joined by one of their old war-time sparring partners, *Volage*.

In 1946 the Flotilla spent some time patrolling the eastern Mediterranean, intercepting shipping carrying illegal immigrants to Palestine. On 22 October there occurred one of the best-known clashes of the Cold War, the so-called 'Corfu Incident'. *Saumarez*, following the cruiser *Mauritius*, and *Volage* steaming astern of the cruiser *Leander*, entered the northern opening of the Medri channel, an international water-way between the Communist-held Albania and the Greek island of Corfu. At 2.53 pm *Saumarez* struck a mine which caused many casualties and damaged the ship so badly she had to be taken in tow (shades of Stewart Sound) stern first by *Volage*. Just after 4 pm another mine detonated close to *Volage*, wrecking her bows. The tow was taken up again and both ships reached Corfu roads stern-first in the early hours of the 23rd. *Saumarez* was taken to Malta where she stayed until September, 1950, when it was decided she was too badly damaged to be worth repairing. She was towed back to the United Kingdom and broken up at Rosyth. Captain Power later presented Denis Calnan with the little wooden steering wheel he had wielded the night they sank *Haguro*, when he had, in fact, been the first officer of the Supply and Secretariat branch to 'command' one of His Majesty's warships in the presence of the enemy since Lieutenant Stanning, Warburton-Lee's Secretary, in *Hardy* at the first battle of Narvik in April, 1940.

In the early 1950s *Venus*, *Virago*, *Verulam* and *Vigilant* were all converted to Type 15 Anti-Submarine Frigates. They served at various times and for various periods with the Home Fleet, and the Dartmouth Training Squadron, escorting the Royal Yacht, carrying out training cruises, taking part in NATO exercises, visiting many ports around the United Kingdom, western Europe and the West Indies. *Venus* saw some service with the Iceland Fishery Patrol in 1959 and 1961. In August, 1967, she was refitted at Plymouth as a Missile Target Trial Ship stationed at

Pembroke Dock. She was sold to T. Ward Ltd. of Sheffield for breaking up in November, 1972.

Virago served in the Plymouth Training Squadron in 1961, and acted as training ship for new entries into the Navy until 1963. In June, 1965, she was towed to the Gareloch and sold to Shipbreaking Industries, at Faslane. *Verulam* was broken up at Newport in 1972. *Vigilant* also served in the Dartmouth Training Squadron with *Venus*. Like *Virago*, she was sold to Shipbreaking Industries in June, 1965.

Of the men who played the greatest part in sinking *Haguro*, only Power reached flag rank and hoisted his flag at sea (although Midshipman Godsal is now a Captain—the only man there that night still serving in the Navy). Bromley, Argles and White were promoted to Captain and retired in that rank, as did Stobie. Midshipman John Robathan also retired as Captain. De Chair was not promoted further and retired as Commander, as did Meryon, Parkinson, Tyers and Robins. Knollys retired as a Lieutenant Commander.

The RNVR and 'hostilities only' men returned to pick up the threads of their lives. Surgeon Lieutenant Evans went into practice as a GP near Manchester. Burns returned to his family and business connections in Liverpool. Fuller also became a business man in the north-west. Norman Poole went back to the Midlands and became chief work study officer in an engineering firm near Wolverhampton. 'Spud' Yates became a blast furnace man and then a steel mill operator.

When they retired and faced the uncertainties of civilian life, the naval officers found themselves employment with professional resourcefulness. Robathan joined Rolls-Royce; de Chair became Master of the Outward Bound Training Schooner *Prince Louis* at the Moray Sea School, Burghead and then became Development Officer for the Hertfordshire Association of Boys' Clubs; Tyers worked for the National Trust and then as Secretary to an old people's housing society in Cheltenham; Knollys became first a printer and then a painter.

Only one man went on upwards—Lofty Power himself. For a time after the war, when a kind of weariness set in, he contemplated resigning from the Navy and retiring to live in South Africa. But the Navy had too strong a hold on him, or powerfully persuasive forces were at work, to convince him that the highest ranks in the Service were possible for him. After the first six months of 1946 at the Admiralty as Deputy Director of Plans, Captain Power went to *Osprey*, the anti-submarine school and headquarters of the asdic world at Portland, where almost his first action was to recommend the establishment's immediate closure unless several reforms were carried out. In July, 1950, he was appointed in command of the fleet carrier *Indomitable* and made a spectacular first arrival at Gibraltar, when *Indomitable* rammed the flagship *Vanguard*'s stern lightly, causing slight damage to both ships, while coming alongside the jetty astern of her. The C-in-C, Admiral Sir Philip Vian, was actually away in another ship. He signalled: 'Tell *Indomitable* not to be so impulsive.'

Captain Power was then invited by the new C-in-C designate, Admiral Mountbatten, to be his Chief of Staff. He accepted this appointment in May, 1952, as he had accepted all his staff billets, reluctantly, but in fact the partnership worked well and he enjoyed it. He was promoted Rear-Admiral in July, 1953. As Chief of Staff, Admiral Power played a large part in the setting up of a NATO headquarters in the Mediterranean.

In April 1954, Admiral Power became Senior Naval Member of the Directing Staff of the Imperial Defence College, and then in 1956 was Flag Officer Aircraft Carriers, with a NATO agglomerate title COMCARSTIGRUTWO (Commander of Carrier Strike Group Two) flying his flag in *Eagle*, *Bulwark*, *Albion* or *Ark Royal* as occasions warranted and as carriers were available. In November, 1956, he commanded the Anglo-French Squadron of five carriers during Operation MUSKETEER, the Anglo-French landings at Suez. Whatever MUSKETEER's political uncertainties and controversies, the Fleet Air Arm's part was a model of modern air strike practice, where the carrier's air groups joined the RAF in quelling the shore-based Egyptian air forces in less than 24 hours, and establishing complete air superiority over the whole Nile delta. For his service at Suez Admiral Power was awarded the Croix de Guerre.

In October, 1957, Power became Deputy Chief of Naval Staff and Fifth Sea Lord, with especial responsibility for the Fleet Air Arm. During his tenure of office he was largely responsible for obtaining for the Navy the Hawker Siddeley Buccaneer strike aircraft. In 1958 he was awarded a KCB and became C-in-C Portsmouth and Allied C-in-C Channel. This was his last appointment, during which he fathered the concept of the present sea training and work-up organisation at Portland. He was promoted full Admiral in July, 1960, and retired in 1962. He now lives in retirement in Yarmouth, Isle of Wight.

Survivors of *Haguro* had a reunion, attended by some of their wives, in May, 1974. But the survivors of the 26th Destroyer Flotilla have never had a reunion, although for all of them it was the greatest night of their lives. Whatever the books and the dispatches and the newspaper cuttings may say, those who were there remember it all on a personal level. As a ship's writer, Alan Parsons knew most of the ship's company in *Saumarez*, through handling their queries on pay lists and service documents. He knew Elliott and Hendren who died in *Saumarez*' boiler-room, 'I can recall what they looked like and usually on Armistice Day I try to think of those two chaps'.

SOURCES

Printed:

Burma's Navy, by Directorate of Information Bureau, Rangoon, 1946, Captain Jack Broome, DSC RN: 'Nocturne in V Minor', *Make a Signal!* (Putnam, 1955).

Commander Denis Calnan, RN: 'It Was Quite Simple: We Were To Sink Her', *Freedom's Battle*, Volume I: The War at Sea 1939–45, edited by John Winton (Hutchinson, 1967).

Charles Causley: 'Demobilisation Leave', *Union Street* (Hart-Davis, 1960).

Fleet Poetry Broadsheet, No. 4, August 1945 (Naval Headquarters, Colombo, Ceylon).

Lieutenant-Commander Shizuo Fukui: *The Japanese Navy—At The End of WW2*, (WE Inc., Old Greenwich, Connecticut, 1947).

Lieutenant John Gritten RNVR: 'Our "Fish" Bite A Jap Cruiser', *The Times of Ceylon Sunday Illustrated*, May 27, 1945.

John Gritten: 'They Misfired—to Prevent Another Massacre?', *Morning Star*, 11 February, 1970.

Major General S. Woodburn Kirby, CB, CMG, CIE, OBE, MC: *The War Against Japan*, Volume V (HMSO, 1969).

Lieutenant C. H. H. Knollys, DSC, RN: 'Nocturne in V Minor', Broadcast over SABC, Capetown, Monday, 18 June, 1945 (Knoxprint, Durban).

Vice-Admiral The Earl Mountbatten of Burma, KG, PC, GCSI, GCIE, GCVO, KCB, DSO: *Report to the Combined Chiefs of Staff by the Supreme Allied Commander South-East Asia 1943–1945* (HMSO, 1951).

Naval Historical Branch, Staff History of Operations of the East Indies Fleet, (in Volume VI of Staff History of War at Sea, 1939–1945).

Bruce Page: 'Blind Faith', *Sunday Times*, 31 August, 1975.

Captain S. W. Roskill, DSC RN: The War at Sea 1939–1945, Volume III, *The Offensive*, Part II (HMSO, 1961).

Senshi Sosho, Official Japanese History of the War, Volume 54.

Tactical and Staff Duties Division (Historical Section), *Burma 1941–1945 Naval Operations* (Naval Staff, Admiralty, SW1, 1948).

F. W. Winterbotham, CBE; *The Ultra Secret* (Weidenfeld & Nicolson, 1974).

John Winton: *The Forgotten Fleet* (Michael Joseph, 1969).

Documents in the Public Record Office:

ADM 199/116 Operations DUKEDOM and MITRE, search for Japanese cruiser *Haguro*, May 1945 (M.06514/45, M.06887/45, and M.07066/45).

ADM 199/168 Operations SUFFICE and TRAINING, destroyer sweeps in the Indian Ocean, February, 1945, and ONBOARD and TRANSPORT, anti-shipping sweeps, March, 1945.

ADM 199/192 Operation STACEY, Photo-reconnaissance, February/March, 1945.

ADM 199/193 Operation BISHOP, Covering force operations for the assault on Rangoon, and GABLE, attack on Japanese leaving Rangoon (M.05523/45 and M.05555/45).

ADM 199/196 Eastern Fleet Weekly State.

ADM 199/275 Naval Operations in the Far East.

ADM 199/340-1, Naval Operations in the Far East, Operations PENZANCE and PASSBOOK, April, 1945, Operation DRACULA, Assault on Rangoon, 2 May, 1945 (M.059165/45 and M.09253/45).

ADM 199/740 Operation ZIPPER, landings at Port Swettenham and Port Dickson, September, 1945.

ADM 199/846 Operation DUKEDOM, anti-shipping sweep in the Indian Ocean, May, 1945.

ADM 199/1057 Operations SUNFISH and BALSAM, photo-reconnaissances, April/June, 1945.

ADM 199/1457 C-in-C East Indies War Diary January–June, 1945 (T.S.D. 3183/45–3189/45).

ADM 199/1870 Patrol Reports, HMS *Scythian*.

ADM 199/1873A Patrol Reports, HMS *Subtle*.

ADM 199/1875 Patrol Reports, HMS *Statesman*.

ADM 199/2317 War Diary Summary 1 May–15 May, 1945.

ADM 199/2318 War Diary Summary 16 May–31 May, 1945.

ADM 223/23 Japanese Intelligence Summaries, OIC/SIJ 176–314.

ADM 223/58 DRACULA Diary.

Unprinted:

William B. Black: Narrative of the sinking of *Haguro*, in MS, 1976.

Commander Denis Calnan, RN: 'Action in the Andamans', in MS, 2 June, 1968.

Commander Graham de Chair, DSC RN: 'Notes From Memory', HMS *Venus*—East Indies Fleet, 1945, in MS, 4 September, 1967.

Lieutenant-Commander Michael Fuller, DSC RNVR; 851 Squadron Diary, 1943–1945, 851 Squadron Line Book.

Captain John Robathan RN; Diary as a Midshipman in HMS *Venus*, 1945.

Naval Historical Branch, Summary of Service, for *Saumarez* (November, 1971), *Venus* (January, 1978), *Virago* (January, 1978), *Vigilant* (February, 1973) and *Verulam* (n.d.).

Letters, comments, signals, photographs, reminiscences, reports of proceedings, diaries, and much other assistance, from Admiral Sir Manley Power, KCB, CBE, DSO and Bar, and those who were there, including Norman Poole, DSM, Jock Yates, CGM, Commander Peter Meryon, DSC and Bar, Captain L. W. L. Argles, CBE, DSC, Commander H. G. D. de Chair, DSC and Bar, Commander D. Calnan, Captain A. J. R. White, DSC, Captain D. H. R. Bromley, DSC, Commander R. Parkinson, DSC, Lieutenant-Commander C. H. H. Knollys, DSC, Michael Fuller, DSC, Commander A. S. Tyers, DSC, Kenneth Marshall, A. B. Dorme, Captain Walter Godsal, Harry Cater, Ted Tyler, John Pocock, Commander the Rev. Julian Richards, Alan Parsons, J. G. V. Burns, Robert Sandford, and Admiral Sir Geoffrey Oliver, GBE, KCB, DSO.

INDEX

The following abbreviations have been used:

HMIS	His Majesty's Indian Ship
RAF	Royal Air Force
RCNVR	Royal Canadian Naval Volunteer Reserve
RIN	Royal Indian Navy
RNAS	Royal Naval Air Service
RNR	Royal Naval Reserve
RNVR	Royal Naval Volunteer Reserve
R.NETH.N.	Royal Netherlands Navy
RNZNVR	Royal New Zealand Naval Volunteer Reserve

Atoll War, 14
Attu, 111
Australia, 8, 22
Avenger, (Grumman TBF/TBM), 44, 53, 57, 66, 78–81, 83, 87, 89, 90, 92–96, 105, 113, 146, 147
Aves Island, 32
Ayerbangis Bay, 47

B-29 (Boeing B-29 Superfortress), 44
Baker, Lieutenant-Commander C. W., 149
Banka Strait, 154
'Banquet', Operation, 16
Baronga Island, 35
Bataan Peninsula, 11
Batavia, 8, 154
Batjan, 111
Batu Islands, 153
Begum, see British Fleet (aircraft carrier)
Bellona, see British Fleet (cruiser)
Bengal, Bay of, 53
Bergen, 96
Bergol, U.S. submarine, 27
Besugo, U.S. submarine, 27
Biak, 111
Biggs, Captain H., 29, 42, 43, 156
Binin River, 9
'Bishop', Operation, 52–55
Bismarck, German battleship, 79
Bismarcks, The (Outer Japanese Defence Barrier), 14
Blackburn Skua, *see* Skua
Boeing B-29 Super Fortress, *see* B-29
Bofors gun, 31, 32, 125, 127, 129, 140–2, 148
'Bogey' (unidentified radar contact), 54, 65, 70, 147–9
Bombay, 11
'Boomerang', Operation, 16
Borneo, 28
Boston, Massachusetts, 78
Bowden, Sub-Lieutenant W. R. P. (RNVR), 81–4, 88, 90
Brien, Ordinary Seaman Paddy, 114
BRITISH FLEET
British Pacific Fleet, formation of, 21; strike on Pangkalanberandan, 22; strike on Palembang, 22
British Pacific Ocean Force, 14
Eastern Fleet, 10–20; largest Admiralty could assemble, 20; lack of submarines, 13; 4th submarine flotilla, 13; fleet strength increased, 14; Operation 'Cock-pit', 15; strike on Sabang, Surabaya and Wonokrono, 15; role during Battle of Philippine Sea, 15; Operation 'Crimson', 16; Operation 'Boomerang', 16; role of submarines, 17; living conditions in submarines, 18; fighting conditions in submarines, 19; partially disbanded to form British Pacific Fleet, 21
East Indies Fleet, 21–56; strength at formation, 22; anti-shipping sweeps in Andaman Sea ('Club runs'), 29; Operation 'Suffice', 29; Operation 'Training', 29; Operation 'Transport', 30–5; behaviour of survivors of convoy attack, 38–42; Operation 'Penzance', 42; Operation 'Passbook', 42; Operation 'Zipper', 43, 50, 156, 157; photo-reconnaissance, 43; Operation 'Roger', 44, 50; Operation 'Stacey', 44; Operation 'Sunfish', 43, 45; 808 Squadron, 45; Operation 'Gable', 49; Operation 'Dracula', 50–2, 55, 57; covering of Operation 'Dracula' in Operation 'Bishop', 52, 53; Destroyer Flotilla (3rd), 162; Destroyer Flotilla (11th), 29, 149; Destroyer Flotilla (16th), 94; Destroyer Flotilla (23rd), 99; Destroyer Flotilla (26th), 1, 2, 41, 60, 66, 76, 86, 88, 90, 93, 96–100, 103, 121, 145–50, 161, 165
SHIPS
Aircraft Carriers: Albion, 164; *Ameer*, 44, 45, 155; *Ark Royal*, 164; *Begum*, 15, 79; *Bulwark*, 164; *Eagle*, 164; *Emperor*, 43, 45, 52, 57, 60, 66, 69, 70, 72, 78, 80, 82, 83, 98–91, 94, 96, 146, 147, 155; *Empress*, 44, 45, 53; *Formidable*, 10, 12, 30, 79; *Glory*, 25; *Hermes*, 10, 11; *Hunter*, 52, 60, 65, 83, 89, 147, 148; *Illustrious*, 12, 14, 16; *Implacable*, 99; *Indomitable*, 6, 10, 12, 16, 17, 164; *Khedive*, 43, 45, 52, 60, 70, 146, 149; *Royalist*, 22, 52, 60, 70, 89, 91, 149; *Shah*, 15, 53, 60, 65, 66, 70, 78–80, 82, 90, 149, 147, 158; *Stalker*, 52; *Unicorn*, 14, 15; *Victorious*, 16, 17, 79, 99

172

173

175

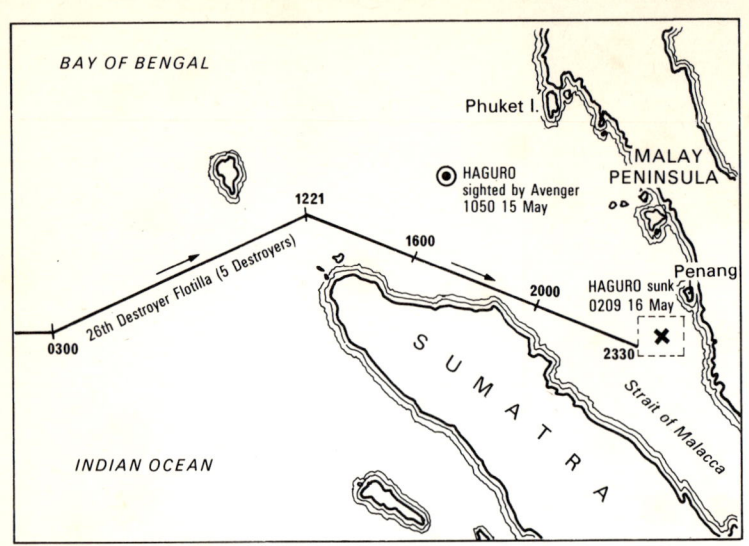

BAY OF BENGAL

Phuket I.

MALAY PENINSULA

HAGURO
sighted by Avenger
1050 15 May

1221

1600

2000

26th Destroyer Flotilla (5 Destroyers)

0300

Penang

HAGURO sunk
0209 16 May

2330

S U M A T R A

Strait of Malacca

INDIAN OCEAN

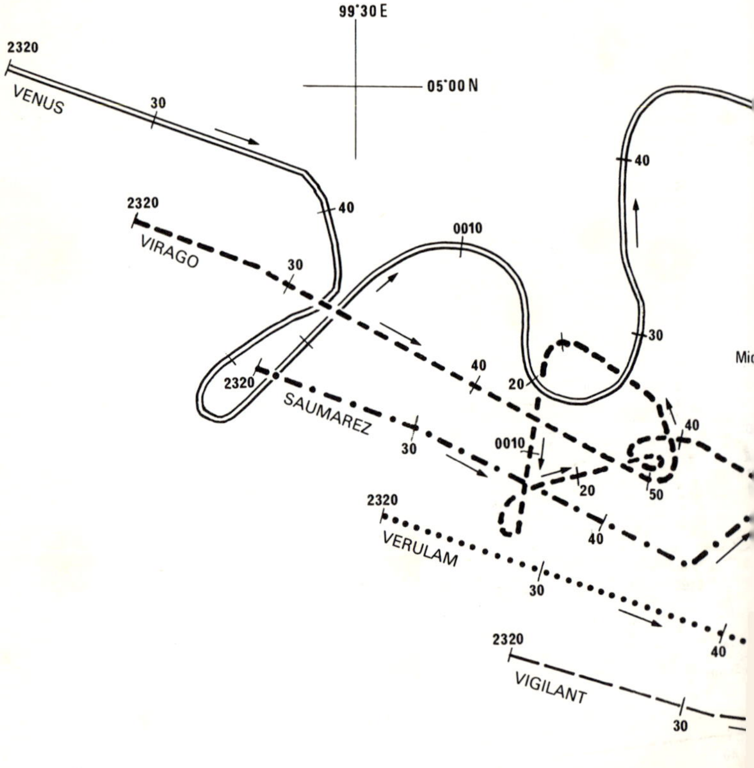

99°30 E

05°00 N

2320
VENUS

30

2320
VIRAGO

30

40

0010

40

30

40
20

2320
SAUMAREZ

30

0010

2320
VERULAM

20

40

30

40

50

40

2320
VIGILANT

30

40

30

Mid